GOD's ONEs
Living in the Lord

so-what ponderings for the
BAPTIZED

including the folks in the
Generous Single Vocation

Stephen Joseph Wolf

idjc.org

God's Ones
Copyright □ 2017
Stephen Joseph Wolf
All rights reserved. No part of this book may be copied
or reproduced in any form or by any means without the
Written permission of the publisher, except for the inclusion
of brief quotations in a review.

Scripture texts in this work unless otherwise indicated
are taken from the *New American Bible, revised edition*, □ 2010,
1991, 1986, 1970 Confraternity of Christian Doctrine, Inc.,
Washington, DC. All Rights Reserved.

Songs are also available in *Fr. Steve's Three-Finger-Chord Ukulele Hymns.*

Stephen Joseph Wolf is a former parish priest, and before that a certified public accountant, who before that worked as a landscaper, desk clerk, laundry worker, janitor, paper boy, and student. He continues to write poems and songs and paint folk art icons and play the ukulele. He lives in Nashville with his husband Billy.

ISBN 978-1-937081-56-0

More six-week books for faith-learning & faith-sharing:

Pondering Our Faith: revised with the new creed
Tree of Life: Saint Bonaventure on the Christ Story
Forty Penances for Spiritual Exercise
The Passion in the Great Story of Jesus
The Resurrection in the Great Story of Jesus
Being Spouses: permanence, fidelity, children & intimacy
God's Money: where faith meets life in the world
Twelve-Step Spirituality for Christians
Anger the Jesus Way
Planning My Own Funeral? (four weeks)

printed and distributed by Ingram Books
IDJC Press   **idjc.org**.

GOD's ONEs: *Living in the Lord*
So-What ponderings for the Baptized
including the folks in the Generous Single Vocation

How to use ***God's Ones***	4
The Generous Single Vocation	5

☐ **One Baptized Into Christ** 7
warrior, king, shaman, lover,
priest, prophet, royal
   Song: *Lord, Your Almighty Word*
   Blessing Sons and Daughters

☐ **Lifegiver Priest** 21
   Song: *To You We Owe Our Hymn of Praise*
   Blessing the Sick

☐ **Soldier Prophet** 35
   Song: *God, Our Refuge and Our Strength*
   Blessing Learners and Teachers

☐ **Footwasher Royal** 53
   Song: *I Know That My Redeemer Lives*
   Blessing Victims of Addiction & Violence

☐ **Beloved Lover** 67
   Song: *Blessed Be*
   Blessing Families

☐ **Vocation Gifted** 85
   Song: *O Breathe on Me O Breath of God*
   Blessing Pilgrims

Sources and For More 104

How to use *God's Ones*

❏ an Individual Seeker

wanting to ponder the generous single vocation:

> Wherever you find yourself drawn,
> linger for pondering, perhaps breathing
> with a particular word or phrase,
> but keep it simple.

❏ Two Friends

reflecting on how God is at work in your vocations:

> Take the time to go slowly,
> and keep it simple.

❏ a Faith Sharing Group

perhaps meeting over six weeks:

> Be sure to include couples, widows and divorced who often have much to add about the single life.
>
> Use what is helpful and ignore the rest; keep it simple.
>
> If someone in the group knows the song, you have a song leader.
>
> Group members can take turns being the *Leader* week to week, but it works best if there is only one *Leader* of each session.
>
> Within each session, group members can take turns being the *Reader*, though no one should be compelled to be a *Reader*.
>
> But keep it simple.

The Generous Single Vocation

God's Ones is intended for all baptized followers of Jesus, but with some emphasis on God's singles.

We all begin life as single people in the world. Single adults include some still open to marriage or a religious vocation, some gay, some straight, some with the charism of celibacy, widows and widowers, separated, divorced, abandoned, unsure, upset, and many who have embraced the *generous single vocation*.

Fr. Bill Bevington, who had baptized me, spoke at the fiftieth anniversary of his ordination about his vocation and vocations in general, calling the single vocation the *dedicated single life*. Having been a single adult for fifteen years before entering seminary, I could not name anything to which I had been dedicated except for family, friends, an addiction to work, and being a lector. There was however an awareness of freedom allowing me an easier generosity than my brothers with small children in the time and energy it took to volunteer at places like the West Nashville homeless shelter. So Fr. Bevington led me to begin thinking of it as *the generous single vocation*.

The *Catechism* in paragraph 2231 states perhaps bluntly that *some forgo marriage in order to care for their parents or brothers and sisters, to give themselves more completely to a profession, or to serve other honorable ends. They can contribute greatly to the good of the human family.* It seems to me there is much more to be said, most of which is relevant to every baptized disciple of Jesus Christ, for singles are more than *forgoers*.

Lord, your al-migh\-ty Word
Cha-os and dark/\-ness heard,
And took their flight;
Hear us we hum-bly pray,
And where the gos-pel day
Sheds not its glo-rious ray, Let there be light!

Sa-vior, you came\ to give
Those who in shad/\-ows live
Heal-ing and sight,
Health to the sick in mind,
Sight to the in-ly blind,
Now to all hu-man-kind   Let there be light!

Spir-it of truth\ and love,
Life-giv-ing, ho/\-ly dove,
Speed forth your flight!
Move on the wa-ter's face
Bear-ing the lamp of grace,
And in earth's sad-dest place, Let there be light!

Ho-ly and bless\-ed Three,
Glo/-rious Trin/\-i-ty, Wis-dom, love, might;
Bound-less as o-cean tide,
Roll-ing in full-est pride,
Through the world far and wide,
                    Let there be light!

Text: Based on Genesis 1:3, *Thou Whose Almighty Word*, John Marriott, 1813, alt.
Music: 664 6664, ITALIAN HYMN (MOSCOW), Felice de Giardini, 1769

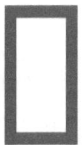

One Baptized Into Christ

*warrior, king, shaman, lover,
priest, prophet, royal*

☐   SONG (from page 6), all together

A member of the group reads **Jeremiah 18:1-6** while others read along in their Bibles.

A member of the group reads **Matthew 3:13-17** while others read along in their Bibles.

A member of the group reads **Mark 1:9-11** while others read along in their Bibles.

Then group members take turns reading the following:

In the winter and spring of 2001, the growing parish where I served as pastor buried several wonderful women and men, including a very unusual number of young men. Funerals and grieving families filled my heart, mind, soul and strength with wonder about what it is to be a Christian, in particular awareness of myself as one Christian man. Pivotal seasons can bring the gift of a deeper walk in the mystery of who God is and who we are called to be.

In the midst of funeral celebrations of life and new life I was working with several Nashville priests and lay faithful around some questions about a Church with fewer priests:
1. What seems to not be attractive about priesthood? Are priests being called into some kind of renewal?
2. What will a Church with fewer priests look like? How will people experience it in parishes?
3. What would a serious vocation campaign look like?

Three: one, two, three. A happy trinity of three questions was comfortable territory. Father, Son, and Spirit. My own baptismal identity in Jesus Christ I saw as **priest**, **prophet** and **king**, from the prayers at the Rite of Baptism.

Pope Saint John Paul II had given us some grounding in his hope-filled work on priestly formation *Pastores Dabo Vobis* (I Will Give You Shepherds, 1992) in which he named levels of formation: **spiritual**, **intellectual**, **pastoral**, and **human**. Four things!

The math confronted me. Four does not equal three. This would not be a great concern for most people. But this priest spent fourteen years as an accountant, bean counter, pinhead, pencil neck, number cruncher, fourteen tax seasons, and good at it. I liked it. But four does not equal three.

Right away I knew this imbalance would find its way into prayer. And in work. And in study. Books on masculine spirituality found their way into my pondering.

I have been most inspired by the heroes of everyday life, but had grown up on knights of the round table, spy novels, and other such. What a gift to watch the real life competition of Hank Aaron and Willie Mays: the things they did with a baseball bat! Teen inspiration came from Bobby Kennedy and Martin Luther King, Jr. But the adult image that made a difference was more than an icon: the person Jesus Christ, fully God and fully man, God on two legs, priest, prophet and king, a living person in a real relationship.

The little book by Franciscan Richard Rohr and Joseph Martos *The Wild Man's Journey* gives a very helpful Christian view of the archetypes of the soul prominent in masculine spirituality. The language of archetypes (*warrior, king, shaman, lover*) and their shadow tendencies, the collective unconscious memory of the human race, the anima and animus of Carl Jung, Joseph Campbell's take on story and ritual; possible feminine archetypes of *mother, mediatrix, companion, amazon* (sound like someone central to Catholic prayer?); all of this was helpful. Mistake me not as an expert on any of it.

Most profound was the simple notion of living a balanced integrated life in imitation of Jesus of Nazareth, the Christ. Yes, this rang a bell on my attention. I can see *warrior*, *king*, *shaman*, and *lover* in Jesus of Nazareth. But could I see them in his baptized disciple I call me?

Steve as a *warrior*? Sort of, with my sainted mother's temper. With minimum imagination visualize the kinds of fights that would happen in a house full of eight sons (no sisters, so let me say what everyone wants to say: *Your poor mother!* My poor mother indeed).

Steve as a *king*? My delay in saying yes to the priesthood happened on God's time, and one of the blessings of it was the time it took to come to some decent awares of the unique set of gifts God has given me. It seems God used public accounting, of all things, to get me ready.

Steve as a *shaman*? What can I say, except that I am a parish priest?

Steve as a *lover*? I'll grant you, this one is a toughie. One reason I feel called to be celibate is that I know how selfish I am. I'll keep taking this to prayer, along with the holier motivations.

Warrior, King, Shaman, Lover.

Priest, Prophet, and King.

Here were images looking for balance.

ARCHTYPES OF THE SOUL	BAPTISMAL IDENTITY
Warrior	Priest
Royal	Prophet
Shaman	Royal
Lover	?

What about my accounting homework? The imbalance is still there. Sneer if you wish but show me a better way to make sense of things, and then reflect on what you may have done in your lifework or love life to be taught your best way to arrive at a *model* or *paradigm* that makes sense to you. But what about my accounting homework? Don't let the debits and credits intimidate you.

OK, some of these line up just fine. Royal = Royal. Shaman and Priest, though not the same thing, share functional similarity. Do either Warrior or Lover match up with Prophet? I went back and forth in my usual slow-thinking way. Prophets generally do not have an easy life, and that corresponds to the life of a Warrior. But if Prophets speak the word that God wants certain people in a particular time and place to hear, then would that not in the end flow out of God's universal love? Maybe. Maybe.

Funerals of good people came, one following another over about six months: a husband and father of five in his forties, two older women, a forty-one year old son and brother and father, a seventeen year old poet and lover of soccer, another husband and father of five in his forties, a nineteen year old racing through life, and an eleven year old battler of cancer.

Taking a hike in the midst of it all, pausing to ponder on a dry creek bed, this *accountant-turned-priest* saw what is called in the profession a "one-legged" (three syllables) journal entry, which is how to fix books out-of-balance once you figure out why. I needed a credit entry without a debit.

Name of Account:
Baptismal Identity

Debit	Credit
	Beloved

A one-legged journal entry must have a good explanation. The source for this one is the words from the heavens at the baptism of Jesus,

> ***This is my <u>Beloved Son</u>,***
> ***with whom I am well pleased***   Matthew 3:17

or the more direct,

> ***<u>You</u> are my Beloved Son;***
> ***with <u>you</u> I am well pleased.***   Mark 1:11; Luke 3:22

With no corresponding debit, this puts things in balance. After much prayer and reflection, may I suggest a further refinement of our identity in the Baptism of Jesus the Christ, Priest, Prophet, King, and Beloved:

ARCHTYPES OF THE SOUL	JESUS THE CHRIST	OUR BAPTISMAL IDENTITY
Shaman	Priest	Lifegiver Priest
Warrior	Prophet	Soldier Prophet
Royal	Royal	Footwasher Royal
Lover	Beloved	Beloved Lover

Before taking these identities one at a time, let's try to account for them all in a kind of *balance sheet* of language we like to use in the Church. (Laugh with me at how fourteen years as an accountant led me to think in columns and rows.)

All words have layers of meaning, so feel free to dispute my arrangement of the rows. Indeed, to ponder and discuss them is the reason I offer them.

Read each column on page 15, top to bottom, one at a time. Does one column describe you more than the others? Are there any rows you want to edit?

missionary cross

a   from the U.S. Bishop's document on Stewardship, 1992
b   areas of Catechesis (teaching the faith)
c   *Called and Gifted for the Third Millennium*, U.S. Bishops, 1995
d   Mark 12:30, our whole being, called to love God
e   1st Corinthians 13:13, *but the greatest of these is love...*
f   Hosea 2:21-22; 4:1, what God is looking for
g   Song refrain of *We Are Called*, by David Haas, based on Micah 6:8, GIA Publications, 1988
h   four most-googled topics, per Thomas Friedman
i   *Pastores Dabo Vobis*, priestly formation per Pope John Paul II
j   experience of the early Church (Greek)
k   experience of the early Church (English)
l   Sirach 39:26, necessities of life
m   *The Rule of St. Benedict*, monastic life
n   the Gospel narratives of the Eucharist (see Matthew 26:26)
o   *Called, Formed and Sent*, by Richard Rohr, NADD, 2002
p   the Cardinal Virtues
q   Fullness of the archetypes per Max Oliva, below, pg 138
r   Archetypes of the mature female, ToniWolff, see footnote *The Masculine Spirit*, Oliva, Ave Maria Press, 1997, pg. 152
s   Nicene Creed, the marks of the Church
t   John 14:6, a self-identification of Jesus
u   Luke 14:13, those unable to reciprocate hospitality
v   *The Divine Image*, poem by William Blake
w   the four cultures of the West, John O'Malley, Harvard, 2005
x   Lenten practices
y   *Reclaiming the Body in Christian Spirituality*, T. Ryan, editor
z   Revelation 5:9, from the canticle of Tuesday Evening Prayer
aa   Vocations
bb   The Catherine of Siena Institute www.siena.org: stages of a Christian life: seeker◦ disciple◦ minister◦ apostle

ONE BAPTIZED INTO CHRIST

A BAPTIZED BALANCE SHEET

	Lifegiver **Priest**	**Soldier** **Prophet**	**Footwasher** **Royal**	**Beloved** **Lover**
a	MYSTERY	MISSION	CREATION	VOCATION
b	Worship	Word	Service	Community
c	*holiness*	*ministry*	*maturity*	*community*
d	HEART	MIND	STRENGTH	SOUL
e	hope	faith	charity	love
f	Mercy	Fidelity	Justice	Knowing God
g	*walk humbly with God*	*act in justice*	*serve one another*	*love tenderly*
h	God	Professional Wrestling	Jobs	Sex
i	**spiritual**	**intellectual**	**pastoral**	**human**
j	LEITURGIA	MARTYRIA	DIAKONIA	KOINONIA
k	(liturgy)	(witness)	(service)	(communion)
l	water	fire	iron	salt
m	Prayer	Study	Work	Daily Life
n	TAKEN	BROKEN	BLESSED	GIVEN
o	formed	sent	gifted	called
p	PRUDENCE	FORTITUDE	JUSTICE	TEMPERANCE
q	*compassionate shaman*	*honest warrior*	*good king*	*responsible lover*
r	mediatrix	amazon	mother	companion
s	HOLY	APOSTOLIC	CATHOLIC	ONE
t	*I am*	*the truth*	*the way*	*the life*
u	poor	blind	crippled	lame
v	mercy	peace	pity	love
w	*academic*	*prophetic*	*humanistic*	*artistic*
x	prayer	fasting	mercy	charity
y	believers	individual	social	earth
z	tribe	tongue	nation	people
aa	*holy-life*	*true-life*	*life-work*	*love-life*
bb	Seeker	Disciple	Apostle	Minister

QUESTIONS FOR CONSIDERATION

1. Most of the words on *A Baptized Balance Sheet* on page 15 can describe Jesus.
   How might *balance* matter to one of his baptized disciples?

2. What does our culture say about
   religious people,
   truth tellers,
   power users,
   and lovers?

3. We all begin as single Christians.
   Between the baptism and anointing of an infant, the baptizer prays,

   *God the Father of our Lord Jesus Christ
   has freed you from sin, given you
   a new birth by water and the Holy Spirit,
   and welcomed you into his holy people.
   He now anoints you with the chrism of salvation.
   As Christ was anointed* **Priest**, **Prophet**, *and* **King**,
   *so may you live always as a member of his body,
   sharing everlasting life.*

   Of *lifegiver priest, soldier prophet,
   footwasher royal,* or *beloved lover,*
   which might best describe me?

4. Single people are often left to feel
   as if they have failed as human beings
   by being uncoupled.
   What could be done about this?

5. Of *priest, prophet, royal,* or *lover,*
   do any seem to least describe me?
   Might there be an invitation
   in this awareness?

6. The four archetypes have been described as
   universal. Are feminine archetypes such as
   mediatrix, companion, mother, and *amazon*
   also helpful? Have any others come to mind?
   How might these apply to an integrated man?

6. Can I think of a concrete way to seek a *balance*
   in my baptismal identity?

7. Ponder whether one of these is surfacing:

   - a seed planted

   - a memory provoked

   - a question raised

   - an action prompted

> Allow a minute for silent pondering,
> and then the group may discuss the ponderings
> (restraining any urge to *fix* anybody).

When time is up:

CLOSING PRAYER
BLESSING SONS AND DAUGHTERS

LEADER

We read in the gospel of Luke, Luke 18:15-17

People were bringing even infants to Jesus that he might touch them, and when the disciples saw this, they rebuked them. Jesus, however, called the children to himself and said, 'Let the children come to me and do not prevent them; for the kingdom of God belongs to such as these. Amen, I say to you, whoever does not accept the kingdom of God like a child will not enter it.'

The gospel of the Lord.

ALL **Praise to you, Lord Jesus Christ**

Brothers and sisters, let us praise our God
who has made us children of God by adoption.

*GROUP MEMBERS TAKE TURNS READING
THE INTERCESSIONS*

Loving Abba, you so loved the world that you gave your only Son; keep in your loving embrace all your sons and daughters reborn in baptism:

ALL **Abba, watch over all your children.**

Your favor rested fully on the Son you loved;
may each one of us successfully carry out the
responsibilities entrusted to us in the world
and in the Church:
> ALL   *Abba, watch over all your children.*

As your Son was to grow in wisdom, age and
favor, you placed him in the tender care of Mary
and Joseph; may all your children grow to the
full maturity of Christ:
> ALL   *Abba, watch over all your children.*

You show a special love for those who are alone
and abandoned; through the help of the Christian
community let all children who are deprived of a
family's love know that you are their Father:
> ALL   *Abba, watch over all your children.*

ALL

**Lord Jesus Christ,
you loved children so much that you said,**
Whoever welcomes a child welcomes me.
**Watch over your brothers and sisters whom
you have blessed with the grace of baptism.
As you were anointed Priest, Prophet and King,
so may we live always as members of your Body
sharing everlasting life.**

Our Father . . .

PSALM 65 — GOD's ONEs

To you we owe our hymn of praise,
Bur-dened with sin your peo-ples come.
You hear our prayer, O God of Zi\-on;
Vows kept and bro-ken, made a-new.

Still ov-er-come are we by sin,
Lord you a-lone can par-don them.
Hap-py the cho-sen ones you bring with-in
Your tem-ple court with good things giv'n.

You an-swer us with awe-some deed,
Jus-tice and hope to ends of earth.
You still the roar-ing of the wave and sea;
Set up the moun-tains by your might.

You still the tu-mult of the crowd,
Now east and west re-sound with joy.
Peo-ple in lands and is-lands far a-way,
See-ing your mar-vel stand in awe.

You vis-it earth and wa-ter her,
Ma-king a-bun-dant streams of life.
God's fer-tile earth pre-pared is blessed in rain,
God's world sup-plied for fields of grain.

Lord, you are hope for all the earth,
You hear the hum-ble sing your praise.
Choose us a-gain, pour out your Spir-it free;
Bear fruit in us that all may see.

Text: Psalm 65, 2003, tribute to the priesthood of George Rohling
Music: JESU DULCIS MEMORIA, LM; Model 1
Popular melody for: *O Radiant Light, O Sun Divine*

Lifegiver Priest

Learn the meaning of the words,
I desire mercy... Matthew 9:13

▢ SONG (from page 20), all together

Keeping a finger on this page, go to PAGE 15
and take turns reading down the *Lifegiver Priest* column.

A member of the group reads **Luke 5:1-11**
while others read along in their Bibles. *(I will make you...)*

A member of the group reads **John 20:19-23**
while others read along in their Bibles. *(in the upper room)*

LEADER And we read in the book of Wisdom,
11:21-12:1

Great strength is always present with you;
who can resist the might of your arm?
Indeed, before you the whole universe
is like a grain from a balance,
or a drop of morning dew come down upon the earth.
But you have mercy on all,
because you can do all things;
and you overlook sins for the sake of repentance.
For you love all things that are
and loathe nothing that you have made;
for you would not fashion what you hate.

Wisdom 11:21—12:1, continued

How could a thing remain, unless you willed it;
or be preserved, had it not been called forth by you?
But you spare all things, because they are yours,
O Ruler and Lover of souls,
for your imperishable spirit is in all things!

The word of the Lord.   ALL   **Thanks be to God**

Then group members take turns reading the following:

In the movie *Schindler's List*, Schindler shares with his new accountant how his father had told him that every successful person needs a good doctor, a clever accountant, and a forgiving priest. Having been an accountant and now a parish priest, I am forced to ignore this odd consolation that only the doctor had to be good!

Somebody has to carry the mysteries. It seems a challenge for most Christians to see ourselves as priests, but somebody has to carry the mysteries. Who can be worthy? Everyone? Nobody? God is God and I am not! There it is: a lesson all people have to learn. God is God and I am not. Still, somebody has to carry the mysteries. If none of us is worthy, is it enough to be willing? Saint Paul wrote to the Corinthians, ***thus should one regard us: as servants of Christ and stewards of the mysteries of God.***   1 Corinthians 4:1

In the Catholic tradition, we speak of the *priesthood of believers* or the *priesthood of the baptized*. Every baptized follower of Jesus Christ is a priest of Jesus Christ. Though not the same as being ordained a priest in the sacrament of Holy Orders, this common priesthood of the baptized is no less real.

In *Secular Sanctity*, Edward Hays wrote, *There is not a single vocation among us which was not once a priestly one - father, mother, soldier, doctor, teacher, nurse, artist, builder of houses and planter of seeds - all of them were ordained by God.* Secular Sanctity, pg. 143

One picture of the Christian life that stays with me is imagining carrying a bucket of holy water, sprinkling people and places and things all through the Christian journey. We have a sanctifying role in God's plan; God uses us in making creation holy. If you have experienced the healing presence of a friend or family member then you have been sprinkled from his or her bucket of holy water.

The archetype of the priest is the Magician or the Shaman, one who bears the special or even secret knowledge. This makes me uncomfortable, and perhaps it should. At a going-away-to-the-seminary party, one friend said, "You will learn things the rest of us can never know." My discomfort here is that I also know that we are as sick as our secrets. To the person not yet initiated into that deepness of reality, from the outside, I see how it can look secretive. Perhaps the core truth here is that to acknowledge our priestliness is to live in an ever deeper way, aware that reality includes more than what we see, touch, smell, taste, and hear.

For sure, being in touch with reality includes seeing, hearing, touching, smelling and tasting. And most true mystics have developed well in these. But there is a reality beyond our senses. Call it the yet unknown, or the place within where God dwells in us, the infinite, or the transcendent. See mystery in the voice of a baby crying or at the breast of a nursing mother, or the capacity to repair a tool, or friends apologizing to each other, how fog forms a hiding place and cold herds us to connection in cramped space and hot weather slows us down and rain makes even people with leakproof skin pick up the pace.

Be warned: each archetype has negative expressions called "shadows," when the archetype is either suppressed or too dominant. The Fool, one shadow of the Shaman, will pretend there is no God, or wish there were no God. Though every disciple is given power by the Holy Spirit, the Fool does not know his or her own gifts, and does not even ask for awareness of illusions or human limitations. Manipulators, the other Shaman shadow, may use smoke with mirrors to trick people into the unholy, but more often just to get their own way.

The *lifegiver priest* avoids forcing people to do things his or her way, but rather assists people in discerning and doing what God wants done. This calls for a trust in God that can make all the difference, that when one is in touch with God's desire for him or her, that one is at the same time in touch with the inmost, deepest, most honest desire of that one for the self. And vice versa. So a *lifegiver priest* has to watch his or her motives: *Do I do what I do the Way I do out of love?*

I have settled on the phrase *lifegiver priest* not because people call me *Father*. Strange, is it not, to call *Father* a man who has made a promise to not marry, the promise to chaste celibacy! I can still remember a long drive to visit some friends, shedding painful tears over having given in to the fact that I would not genetically father a child. Every seminarian, every priest has to grieve this loss. It is a real loss, not to be minimized.

Though it can sneak up on me at odd times, having grieved this loss has helped me be more aware of the various ways that a parish priest gives life to the people with whom he shares life.

Perhaps the most striking priestly pose I will ever see was the wife of one of my seven brothers perched awkwardly, kneeling over her four year old son, my nephew after a surgery, simply staying close to him, making sure he knew he was not alone, that he was loved. Hers was a healing presence, true medicine. All my helpless brother Kevin could do was keep lifting to Bunny's neck his son's falling arm.

This priestly pose of my sister-in-law is one reminder to me of Mary as the primary model of what it is to be a priest. Mary pondered, and Mary was present. The apostles, a different model of priesthood, ran away from the cross.

One of my fine spiritual directors helped me to see how Simon Peter reacted to realizing he was in the presence of God. Luke 5:1-11 is a miracle story of a catch of fish that was simply astonishing. When we are graced with awareness that God is God and we are not, we know our sinfulness. The face of Jesus shines light onto my own sin, and I want to do what Simon did: drop to my knees before him and say, *Depart from me, Lord, for I am a sinful man,* as if to say,

Lord, I can see that you have a mission. You have

much good to do. You cannot let me be part of it. If I am part of your mission, it will not go well. I will ruin the whole thing, because I am a sinner. You know it, Lord, and I know it.

How does Jesus respond to Simon's objection? He says, **Do not be afraid...** Imagine Jesus lifting Simon off his knees, signing him with the dignity of being named as a disciple. If I may continue to paraphrase, Jesus communicates to Simon,

You know you are sinner. I know you are a sinner. I call you anyway. Do not be afraid. You will be a catcher of human beings. I will give you the grace to help them to have no fear, but in the meantime, you, yourself, be not afraid.

And what then did Simon do? He and his brother Andrew, with the brothers James and John, they left **everything** and followed him.

The essential verbs for a *lifegiver priest* are to **sanctify** and to **pray** and to **forgive**. The word *forgiveness* as a noun sometimes gives me the creeps. We can walk around and ponder a noun, like a sculpture. But the verb *forgive*, this is something Jesus is calling us to *do*.

One of the funnier moments in the gospels is when Jesus states flatly they must forgive: Seven times? Jesus says, basically over and over, you cannot stop. Forgive. Forgive. And forgive. The reply of the disciples seems to explode from the gut: ***Increase our faith!*** (Luke 17:4). The disciples give a beautiful human response, again to paraphrase,

Well, OK, we will, but you are going to have to increase our faith, because that is the only way this is going to be possible!

The only way possible is by the grace of God.

The Reconciliation ritual, the sacrament availed by Catholics where we experience God's forgiveness in the presence of a priest, is rooted in the lived experience of the people of the Church. In the early centuries, Penance was an embarrassing public ritual. Most of us could have predicted that it would not be used by many people. Then in sixth century Ireland, it seems people going to monks to discuss one-to-one their prayer lives began to confess sinfulness and experience the forgiveness of God in a ritual that developed and spread fairly quickly through Europe.

The Church saw what was happening and recognized in it the real presence of Christ the Risen Lord, and so deemed it a Sacrament. The clear scriptural roots include where Jesus gave Peter the *keys to the kingdom* in Matthew 16:19 and the eighth day appearance in the upper room, John 20:22-23, when Jesus breathed in and onto the apostles the commission to forgive sins.

Friends, as baptized followers of Jesus Christ, priests of Jesus Christ, we too have all been commissioned to forgive sins, if not all sins, certainly those offenses against us.

The child-like spirituality of forgiveness in the inevitable setbacks of life can help us forget our injuries when that is healthy, and avoid self-pity and the slow welling up of resentment. St. Leo the Great

We can refuse to forgive. God has given us the freedom to refuse. We can choose to be enslaved by the unforgiven. But Jesus has breathed onto us the power to forgive. Jesus has given us that grace, and he continues to offer it to us when we need it. And we will always need it.

Lord, keep breathing onto us the power to forgive.
Lord, increase our faith!

To circle back to the basics, the *lifegiver priest* is first of all a ***seeker*** who has been touched by a taste of the divine. There has been an experience, from stargazing or some other way of contemplating creation, some awareness of the presence of God. Perhaps something attractive has been seen in another disciple, and the seeker wants it. This is from the nature of a human, created in the image of God with a *capacity* or a longing for God. Christians are always seekers, always wondering what else the Lord may have in store. And seekers are not always lost. In some ways the pilgrim journey itself is the vocation.

And so the priesthood of a baptized Christian is also about that thing we call prayer, which can be as simple as spending regular time with the One who knows me better than I know myself.

Call to mind your best friend. How did you two happen to become best friends? Would he or she be your best friend if you had not spent so much time together that you became happy to waste time with each other? Here is my favorite definition of prayer: *Wasting time with God.*

Should any of us be surprised to discover that God desires to waste time with us? God is jealous about this in the good sense of the word. But we need not be jealous of God, whose love is infinite!

Lord, increase our faith!

FOR CONSIDERATION

1. Two university professors of business wrote that a good corporation would have a *priest* in its midst. What might they have meant by this? Who might be a *"priest"* where I work?

2. Is there some part of creation onto which God might want me to *"sprinkle"* some holy water?

3. Empowered by their baptisms, spouses *confer* onto each other the sacrament of marriage. How else are they priests to each other?

4. Take a deep breath...
   What difference does it make to know that Jesus is breathing into and onto me the power to forgive?

5. After September 11, 2001, Saint John Paul II said,   *No peace without justice;
       no justice without forgiveness*?
   How does this saying speak to our time:

6. Two prayers to consider:

   Lord, how do you desire that I return praise to you and give thanks for how you bless me?

   Lord, how do you desire that I spend (waste) time with you alone?

7. Sacraments of forgiveness (*Eucharist, Penance, Anointing*) could also be called *priestly* sacraments. What connections do I see between healing and forgiveness?

8. Ponder whether one of these is surfacing:
   - a seed planted   - a question raised
   - a memory provoked   - an action prompted

When time is up:

CLOSING PRAYER
BLESSING THE SICK

LEADER

We read in the gospel of Mark,   _{Mark 6:53-56}

After making the crossing, they came to land at Gennesaret and tied up there. As they were leaving the boat, people immediately recognized him. They scurried about the surrounding country and began to bring in the sick on mats to wherever they heard he was. Whatever villages or towns or countryside he entered, they laid the sick in the marketplaces and begged him that they might touch only the tassel on his cloak; and as many as touched it were healed.

The gospel of the Lord.

    ALL   **Praise to you, Lord Jesus Christ**

LEADER

Brothers and sisters, let us bless the Lord,
who went about doing good and healing the sick.

GROUP MEMBERS TAKE TURNS READING THE INTERCESSIONS

Lord Jesus, you came as healer of body
and of spirit, to cure all our ills:

    ALL   **Lord, comfort the sick with your presence.**

You were a man of suffering,
but it was our sufferings you endured:
> ALL *Lord, comfort the sick with your presence.*

You chose to be like us in all things but sin,
and so assure us of your compassion:
> ALL *Lord, comfort the sick with your presence.*

You experienced human weakness
to deliver us from evil:
> ALL *Lord, comfort the sick with your presence.*

It is your wish that in our own flesh we should
fill up what is wanting in your sufferings
for the sake of your Body, the Church:
> ALL *Lord, comfort the sick with your presence.*

ALL

**Lord Jesus Christ,
who went about doing good and healing all,
we ask you to bless your friends who are sick.
Give them strength in body,
courage in spirit,
and patience with pain.
Let them recover their health,
so that restored to the Christian community
they may joyfully praise your name,
who live and reign for ever and ever.
Our Father . . .**

PSALM 46 — GOD's ONEs
Melody: *All Creatures of Our God and King*

God, our/ ref-uge and our strength,
Ev-er/ pres-ent help in stress.
God is with us, thus we fear not.
Though the\ earth and moun-tains shake,
Deep of\ wa-ters foam and rage,
Moun-tains tot-ter, wa-ter surg-ing,
God of Ja-cob is our strong-hold,
                         God is with - - - us.

Ho-ly/ dwell-ing of our God,
Stream-ing/ riv-er glad-den there
In the cit-y of our ref-uge.
Na-tions\ rage and king-doms fall,
All earth\ trem-bles at the call,
God will help at break of new day,
God of Ja-cob is our strong-hold,
                         God is with - - - us.

"Be still and know that I am God."
Come and/ see the works of God:
Stop-ping war in ev-'ry na-tion,
Break-ing\ weap-on, break-ing spear,
Burn-ing\ bow and ar-mor shield,
Say-ing, "Be still, know your God now,"
God of Ja-cob is our strong-hold,
                         God is with - - - us.

Text: Psalm 46, by Stephen J. Wolf, 2003,
tribute to the priesthood of Joseph E. Wesley
Music: LASST UNS ERFREUEN, LM with alleluias; *Geistliche Kirchengesange*, 1623

Soldier Prophet
What is truth?
Pontius Pilate

☐ SONG (from page 34), all together

Keeping a finger on this page, go to PAGE 15
and take turns reading down the *Soldier Prophet* column.

A member of the group reads **Mark 3:1-6**
while others read along in their Bibles. *(with anger)*

A member of the group reads **Matthew 14:1-20**
while others read along in their Bibles. *(beheading & miracle)*

LEADER And we read in the book of Wisdom,
                                                                           7:22-26

Wisdom, the artisan of all, taught me.
For in her is a spirit intelligent, holy, unique,
manifold, subtle, agile, clear, unstained, certain,
never harmful, loving the good, keen,
unhampered, beneficent, kingly,
firm, secure, tranquil, all-powerful, all-seeing,
and pervading all spirits,
though they be intelligent, pure and very subtle.
For Wisdom is mobile beyond all motion,
and she penetrates and pervades all things
by reason of her purity.

For she is a breath of the might of God
and a pure emanation of the glory of the Almighty;
therefore nothing defiled can enter into her.
For she is the reflection of eternal light,
the spotless mirror of the power of God,
the image of his goodness.
Although she is one, she can do all things,
and she renews everything while herself perduring;
Passing into holy souls from age to age,
she produces friends of God and prophets.

The word of the Lord.   ALL   **Thanks be to God**

Then group members take turns reading the following:

In the gospel of Matthew (14:13), hearing the bad news of the death of his baptizer John, Jesus does what you or I might do. He withdraws in a boat to a deserted place by himself.

A boat is a vehicle over water, and Bible water holds layers of meaning, a symbol of life and chaos, quiet, movement, safety, danger, the stuff of baptism. The waters of the Jordan River had come from these waters of Galilee, where wind and wave could rise and toss a boat about. Life. Death. Uncertainty. And a desert place.

We won't know 'til heaven, but to me it seems that Jesus heard in the news of the Baptist's death his own death coming. Did he know he would die on a cross, in exactly the way it happened? What person this side of heaven can know? But if he had not yet known he would be killed, he did that day.

Fr. Bill Fleming was pastor in my first two years as a priest. He was one of the greats, a teacher of scripture at Nashville's Father Ryan High School for more than a generation of students, and principal for a year, my senior year. I was not blessed to be a student, but many who were testify that he was their best teacher. He was also a great preacher.

A couple of times a year he would challenge Cathedral parishioners:

For what are you willing to die?
For what or for whom would you give up your life?
If there is nothing or no one for whom you would die, are you really alive?

Let me propose this as *the* question for a *soldier prophet*, because once a man or woman can answer that question, then, perhaps only then, can that same man or woman fully live for that person, idea, or whatever it be. My life can be taken from me at any time, but I cannot give up my life for myself, only for another.

And is this not what Jesus did? In the gospel of Luke (9:9) Herod is quoted, *John I beheaded. Who then is this about whom I hear such things?* While Herod continues to wonder and try to see him, Jesus knows who Jesus is and what Jesus is about. He feeds the five thousand, and Peter confesses Jesus is *the Messiah of God*. Jesus predicts his passion, calls followers to take up their cross daily and follow him, is shown transfigured, rebukes another unclean spirit, predicts his passion again, teaches the humility of the least, and then *resolutely determines to journey to Jerusalem* (Luke 9:51).

As Jesus absorbs and processes the news of the death of John the Baptist, and as a prelude to the cross (which Gandhi called a *perfect act of nonviolence*), Jesus sets his face to Jerusalem. He knows what his mission is, knows why he will give up his life, and in that knowing seems to grow in power and freedom. In setting his face to Jerusalem, Jesus fully lives for those for whom he will give up his life, his ultimate free act of love.

I would die for my child, or my spouse! Great! Now you know what your life is about. Now, fully live for your child. Be fully faithfully present and freely attentive, not because you have to, not because it is your duty, not because someone might think better of you. But do it because it is part of the mission of Jesus Christ.

I would die for my country, or my people! Congratulations! Now you know your reason to live. Vote. Be a faithful citizen. Speak the truth with compassion. Do your part to help make your country everything she can be, not because people will thank you, not because you might make money doing it, not because you are the messiah (for that job's already taken). But do it because it is part of the mission of Jesus Christ.

I would die for my God, or my faith! Excellent! Now you know why God made you. Read the inspired text. Teach it to others. Learn everything you can about the Son of God and his mission and tell others about him, not because people will think you are holy, and not because of heaven. But do it because the mission of Jesus Christ has a Church, and you are part of this Body of Christ.

OK. I get *prophet*, but *soldier*? I have always had tremendous respect for the good people who serve in the armed forces, even more now serving in a parish with many military families. But being a *soldier for Christ* never appealed to me. Growing up in the shadow of the Vietnam War may be why *soldier for Christ* did not reconcile with my vision of the person of Jesus.

Then a grace-filled exercise was proposed by Tom, my seminary spiritual director: *Make a pledge to be nonviolent.* So on an October 13, the birthday of my temper-gifted sainted mother Jeanette, I met with a priest and made this peacemaker pledge of the Catholic peace movement *Pax Christi*:

> Recognizing the violence in my heart, yet trusting in the goodness and mercy of God, I pledge for one year to practice the nonviolence of Jesus who taught us in the Sermon on the Mount (Matthew 5):
> *Blessed are the peacemakers, for they shall be called the sons and daughters of God... You have learned how it was said, 'You must love your neighbor and hate your enemy,' but I say to you, 'Love your enemies, and pray for those who persecute you.' In this way, you will be daughters and sons of your Creator in heaven.*
>
> I pledge to carry out in my life the love and example of Jesus
> - by striving for peace within myself and seeking to be a peacemaker in my daily life;
> - by accepting suffering rather than inflicting it;
> - by refusing to retaliate in the face of provocation and violence;
> - by persevering in nonviolence of tongue and heart;
> - by living conscientiously and simply so that I do not deprive others of the means to live;

☐ by actively resisting evil
and working nonviolently to abolish war
and the causes of war from my own heart
and from the face of the earth.

O God, I trust in your sustaining love and believe that just as you gave me the grace and desire to offer this pledge, so you will also bestow abundant grace to fulfill it. Amen.

paxchristiusa.org

Attempting to be nonviolent, I discovered how violent I am, Momma's temper and all. What was this anger all about? Invited to take an honest look at my anger, I went searching for the anger of Jesus. He teaches us to acknowledge our anger as a human emotion, but to do what can be done to keep it from growing. Don't nurture it, but admit it, know it, and let it die of its own emptiness.

If you expect the gospel writers to tell us Jesus was angry, you are correct. If you expect to find it in the story of the turning over of the tables in the Temple, you are incorrect. Jesus was probably angry that day; the tone and the setting suggest it. But the gospel writers do not use the word *anger* there. I sometimes pray with this story, imagining Jesus knows he is going to make everyone else angry, especially the religious leaders, and happy to oblige goes to town having a great old time, the way one friend pushes another friend's buttons for the friend's own good, or just for the fun of it.

The word *anger* is applied to Jesus one time in another setting that has become one of my favorite gospel passages: *Mark's story of the healing of the man with a withered hand. They are in the synagogue on the Sabbath: a worshipping community that includes Jesus, some Pharisees, and this man with a withered hand. Jesus knows they are waiting to accuse him. He invites them with a riddle. They have already been losing these battles of wits, so they refuse to enter into dialogue with him. *Looking around at them with anger, and grieved at their hardness of heart* (Mark 3:5), Jesus owns his emotion.

Jesuit friend Jim Pratt was the first to tell me that the word used for *anger* means that *his bowels turned inward*. In this state Jesus invited the man to hold out his withered hand; the man did and the hand was restored. He was made whole.

Other emotions of Jesus can also be found in the gospel of Mark: pity (1:41), sternness (1:43), groaning (7:34), sighing from the depth of his spirit (8:12), indignant (10:14), and loving (10:21).   NJBC pg. 603

*See *Anger the Jesus Way*, Stephen Joseph Wolf, idjc press, 2017.

Jesus shows me, via the writer of the gospel of Mark, how to deal with my anger: to know I am angry, to admit to myself that I am filled with this emotion, to be honest with myself about its source (the person with whom I am truly angry so that I not lash out at some innocent soul), and then to hold that anger with grief, with compassion, to suffer with the source. Often enough the source is my very self.

The truth is that I cannot ever know what is going on in the heart of another child of God. At best it's a game of guess. On most days I cannot even be certain about what is going on in my own heart, so how could I judge the heart of another? Even when I am most certainly *in the right* and the person bringing rise to my emotion of anger is most certainly *in the wrong*, to judge remains the job of God alone. Only God has all the data.

A little story that may not help at all: A neighboring restaurant manager threatened that cars of parishioners would be towed, just as soon as he got angry enough to do it. When I suggested that since he felt he had given plenty of notice to repeat offending parkers, perhaps he should have the cars towed before he reached the point of anger. That might be the only way people will stop parking where they know they ought not.

He looked at me as if I had three heads and horns. Why would someone, anyone, do something that might offend another without first becoming angry? Because rarely is any situation improved because someone acted on their anger. Anger is a human emotion and hardly ever the best motivator, even against injustice. May our actions be motivated rather by that matrix the prophet Hosea offers, what God is looking for: justice, mercy, fidelity, and knowledge of God.

Gandhi understood this. Martin Luther King, Jr. understood this, the provocative nonviolence of Jesus found in the Sermon on the Mount. I am grateful for teacher Robert Barron for keeping the phrase *provocative nonviolence* in front of us. It suggests a creative stance, a refusal to retaliate that risks being hurt, but which can sometimes draw violence out of people in power, as when puss is drained out of a punctured sore. When bystanders witness unreasoned violence, God's grace has room to work into consciences. God's grace can even reach the one inflicting the pain.

As a student of Jesus' teachings and human ways, Gandhi understood how challenging nonviolence can be. He learned that the most suitable students of nonviolence would often be former soldiers. Knowing the violence within one's own self can enable training toward not-fighting. Many of the soldiers I know seem to have an intuitive sense of the awkward logic of the cross.

My first time at an airport after September 11, 2001 is now an old memory; soldiers were already there. It was something of a shock, and reminded me of seeing Israeli soldiers climb out of a volzwagon beetle, rifles and all, to wait with me at a Jerusalem bus stop. There was something cartoonish about it, yet bizarrely normal, as if their guns were really toolboxes or briefcases. The purpose of the soldiers at that airport and at that bus stop was not to fight but to be ready to keep violence from happening, to assume the risk of standing ready in the breach.

A *soldier prophet* is willing to stand in the breach, silent or speaking the truth, a word that God wants spoken to a particular person or people in a particular time and place, risking that the hearer might not want to hear it and give a rough response. No one seeks to be a prophet, because we usually kill the prophets.

War is hell. Always has been. Always will be. It is true that there will also always be innocent and powerless people in need of protection from people who seek to harm them. Still, war will always mean our human race has failed again.

The shadows of a Warrior are the Sadist, who takes pleasure in the suffering and difficulties of others, and the Masochist, who confuses pain and suffering as the reason for the fight. Richard Rohr reminds us how dangerous is a warrior who has neither king nor true community, like an Indian male elephant exiled from its tribe. The Feast of *Christ the King* on the last Sunday of the liturgical year, just before re-entering the Advent season of the watch and the wait, was added to our calendar a hundred years ago when nationalism was on the rise and endangering world peace.

It concerns me to meet someone who has not yet embraced the grace to name his or her cross. Abuse? Addiction? Anxiety? Broken heart? Chronic pain? Depression? Despair? Disability? Disease? Dusty old hurts? Failures? Limp? Powerlessness? Scars? Selfishness? Stutter? Success? Unclaimed sexuality? The Unforgiven? Pride is the willful refusal to name our cross. Grace is what touches our being willing to try.

If I refuse to name my cross, it will still be there, usually in plain sight of everyone else, perhaps as the cross-plank in the eye of the unaware judger in the fun-poking parable of Luke 6:41 and Matthew 7:4. Sometimes Jesus uses our cartoon imagination to let the truth sink in.

Back to the basics, the *soldier prophet* embraces *discipline*, related to the word ***disciple***, one who is first and foremost a student in training. A disciple learns a way of life, a discipline, the way of Jesus, studying and praying with the person of Jesus.

A disciple always has a teacher, a master. Our master is Christ himself, and the disciple-pose is at his feet. God's innumerable ways of speaking God's love are not new revelations but new articulations of the one Word, if translatable into understandable words, perhaps a one-of-a-kind version of *I made you, I know you, and I love you.*

The child-like spirituality of the prophet begins with *wonder of God and of all things,* beginning with wide-eyed curiosity and delight, at awe before the mystery of God. St. Leo the Great

My favorite definition of a prophet is one who so accurately describes the present that it becomes clear what the future will bring. Simon proclaims in Mark 1:37 a power-truth: Jesus begins his ministry in Galilee, calling two pairs of brothers, and has a tiring day of teaching and healing. He rises before dawn and goes to a deserted place to pray, literally a *desert* place. Simon finds him and speaks this truth: *Everyone is looking for you!* Those are words of a prophet. Everyone is looking for God. Amen. Amen.

FOR CONSIDERATION

1. Consider: one chapter-a-day takes 44 months.

One plan: Begin with the shortest Book (2nd John with 13 Verses) and read through to the longest (Isaiah with 66 chapters). You will find passages to return to often.

PENTATEUCH
- 50 Genesis
- 40 Exodus
- 27 Leviticus
- 36 Numbers
- 34 Deuteronomy

HISTORICAL
- 24 Joshua
- 21 Judges
- 4 Ruth
- 31 1st Samuel
- 24 2nd Samuel
- 22 1st Kings
- 25 2nd Kings
- 29 1st Chronicles
- 36 2nd Chronicles
- 10 Ezra
- 13 Nehemiah
- 14 Tobit
- 16 Judith
- 10 Esther
- 16 1st Maccabees
- 15 2nd Maccabees

WISDOM BOOKS
- 42 Job
- 41 Psalms 1-41
- 31 Psalms 42-72
- 17 Psalms 73-89
- 17 Psalms 90-106
- 44 Psalms 107-150
- 31 Proverbs
- 12 Ecclesiastes
- 8 Song of Songs
- 19 Wisdom
- 51 Sirach

THE PROPHETS
- 66 Isaiah
- 52 Jeremiah
- 5 Lamentations
- 6 Baruch
- 48 Ezekiel
- 14 Daniel
- 14 Hosea
- 4 Joel
- 9 Amos
- 21vs. Obadiah
- 4 Jonah
- 7 Micah
- 3 Nahum
- 3 Habakkuk
- 3 Zephaniah
- 2 Haggai
- 14 Zechariah
- 3 MalachI

THE GOSPELS
- 28 Matthew
- 16 Mark
- 24 Luke
- 21 John
- 28 Acts

PAULINE LETTERS
- 16 Romans
- 16 1st Corinth.
- 13 2nd Corinth.
- 6 Galatians
- 6 Ephesians
- 4 Philippians
- 4 Colossians
- 5 1st Thess.
- 3 2nd Thess.
- 6 1st Timothy
- 4 2nd Timothy
- 3 Titus
- 23vs. Philemon
- 13 Hebrews

CATHOLIC LETTERS
- 5 James
- 5 1st Peter
- 3 2nd Peter
- 5 1st John
- 13vs. 2nd John
- 15vs. 3rd John
- 25vs. Jude
- 22 Revelation

2. *Bear your share of hardship along with me like a good soldier of Christ Jesus. To satisfy the one who recruited him, a soldier does not become entangled in the business affairs of life. Similarly, an athlete cannot receive the winner's crown except by competing according to the rules. The hard working farmer ought to have the first share of the crop.*
   Reflect on what I am saying. (Saint Paul, 2 Timothy 2:3-7a)
   Describe an ideal soldier.
   What is the source of his or her strength?

3. Soldier, Warrior, Police Officer, Defender, Guardian, Peacemaker: It may at first seem odd to call a soldier or a weapon a *peacemaker*: Can it make sense?

4. If the life of a soldier or prophet can be lonely, how does a *soldier prophet* find community?

5. One of the disciplines needed to be a prophet is the courage to speak the word and then the prudence to get out of the way. How is a prophet to know when to speak, when to be silent, and when to stand in the breach?

6. Lord, help me to see why I am alive. For whom or for what would I give up my life? For this now, can I fully live?
   What will that look like?

7. Lord, how do you want to teach and train me to be the *soldier prophet* you want me to be?

8. Ponder whether one of these is surfacing:
   - a seed planted
   - a question raised
   - a memory provoked
   - an action prompted

Allow a minute for silent pondering, and then the group may discuss the ponderings (restraining any urge to *fix* anybody).

When time is up:

CLOSING PRAYER
BLESSING LEARNERS AND TEACHERS

LEADER

We read in Paul's 1st Letter to the Corinthians,

1 Cor 15:1-11

For I received from the Lord what I also handed on to you, that the Lord Jesus, on the night he was handed over, took bread, and, after he had given thanks, broke it and said, "This is my body that is for you. Do this in remembrance of me." In the same way also the cup, after supper, saying, "This cup is the new covenant in my blood. Do this, as often as you drink it, in remembrance of me." For as often as you eat this bread and drink the cup, you proclaim the death of the Lord until he comes.

The word of the Lord.   ALL   **Thanks be to God**

SOLDIER PROPHET

LEADER Brothers and sisters, let us praise the God of wisdom, knowledge, and grace.

GROUP MEMBERS TAKE TURNS READING THE INTERCESSIONS

For all who seek to learn, may the Spirit of God give them wisdom and understanding:
> ALL ***Fill us with your wisdom, Lord.***

For teachers, may they share their knowledge with gentleness, patience, and concern:
> ALL ***Fill us with your wisdom, Lord.***

For those who seek knowledge of this world, may they always pursue God's wisdom:
> ALL ***Fill us with your wisdom, Lord.***

For parents, the first teachers of their children, may their faith and love be an example to us all:
> ALL ***Fill us with your wisdom, Lord.***

ALL **Lord our God, in your wisdom and love you surround us with the mysteries of the universe. In times long past you sent your prophets to teach your laws and to bear witness to your undying love. You sent your Son to teach by word and example that true wisdom comes from you alone. Teach us your ways and lead us to the joys of your kingdom, now and for ever. Amen.**

I know that my Re/-deem-er\ lives;
What com-fort this sweet sen-tence gives!
Liv-ing\ Proph/-et/, Priest\, and\ King;
Liv-ing and while he lives I'll sing.

He lives/ hun-gry/ souls to\ feed,
Liv-ing to help in time of need.
Liv-ing to grant/ us/ rich\ sup\-ply,
Liv-ing to guide us with his eye.

He lives/ qui-et/-ing our\ fears,
Liv-ing to wipe a-way our tears,
Liv-ing to calm/ our/ troubl\-ed\ heart,
Liv-ing all bless-ings to im-part.

He lives/, glo-ry/ to his\ Name!
Liv-ing, my Je-sus, still the same.
Oh, sweet the joy/ this/ sen\-tence\ gives:
"I know that my Re-deem-er lives!"

Text: from Job 19:25-27, Samuel Medley, 1775, altered
Music: DUKE STREET, LM, John Hatton, 1793
Popular melody for: *From All That Dwells Below The Skies*

Footwasher Royal

*If you understand this, blessed
are you if you do it.* John 13:17

☐ SONG (from page 52), all together

Keeping a finger on this page, go to PAGE 15
and take turns reading down the *Footwasher Royal* column.

A member of the group reads **Luke 10:25-37**
while others read along in their Bibles. (*the Good Samaritan*)

A member of the group reads **John 13:1-17**
while others read along in their Bibles. (*footwashing*)

LEADER And we read in the book of Wisdom, 7:1-6

*I too am a mortal, the same as all the rest,
and a descendant of the first one formed of earth.
And in my mother's womb I was molded into flesh
in a ten-month period - body and blood,
from the seed of man,
and the pleasure that accompanies marriage.
And I too, when born, inhaled the common air
and fell upon the kindred earth;
wailing, I uttered that first sound common to all.*

*In swaddling clothes and with constant care
I was nurtured.
For no king has any different origin or birth;
one is the entry into life for all,
and in one same way they leave it.*

The word of the Lord.   ALL **Thanks be to God**

Then group members take turns reading the following:

The Genesis stories get to the point fairly quickly. God creates humanity in the image of God, male and female, both in the divine image (Gen. 1:27). God does this in an earthy way,
*formed ('adam) out of the dust of the ground
and blew into his nostrils the breath of life,
and ('adam) became a living being.*   (Gen. 2:7)
With every intake of the breath of life I can pray praise to the One who made me in the image of God, and tell the thanks that be to God who calls me to grow into the likeness of the Risen Christ.

Psalm 104, a song to praise God our Creator, has found a place in my heart. It reminds me that I am part of God's creation, neither helpless nor omnipotent. Like all creatures, I too will die an earthly death. But God did not make me so that I could die; rather so that I might live and be fully alive. As I breathe, God is still up to something.

Imagine that you have lost your job, and for some reason you are not allowed to work. Tired as most of us usually are, you get a lot of good rest. But still able-bodied, you start to putter around the house looking for something to do. This is how my friend Eric likes to pray, puttering in his backyard garden.

Trappist monk Thomas Merton wrote of Saint Augustine's contention that in the garden Adam and Eve would have done some work, because participating in God's ongoing creation is part of our human nature. They were not sloth slugs, but human, and so would have done some kind of life-giving work. **And the work Adam and Eve would have done in the garden was worship**.

In my tax accounting days as a CPA, Monday morning work almost always felt like punishment for the sins of the entire human race. But there were so many other days when I felt fully alive, in a groove, in my element, doing the things I felt, at that time in my life, God wanted me to do: an accountant bring some order out of chaos, helping people understand and deal with complexities of tax and finance, and helping people set and realize goals.

When we look out only for ourselves, when we live in fear as if we are at war, our work continues to symbolize a people expelled from Eden. When we are using the gifts, talents, and charisms that God has given us to participate in God's creative work, the work we do is worship.

The work for each of us to do is as unique as are we, who are uniquely created in God's image. No two of us have the same exact collection of natural talents, earthly backgrounds, human gifts, or spiritual graces (*that Saint Paul called **charisms**; more on this in chapter 6*).

The great teacher Fr. Larry Hennessey shared an image that surely many of his students use, that when God counts us, God does not tally up one through seven billion whatever, but that God counts us this way: *one, one, one, one, one, one, one, one, one, one, one, one, one, one, one, one, one, one…* For we are each created uniquely in God's image. (Once doing this in a classroom, a little boy ran up to the front with a smile, *"Do me!,"* for I had inadvertently left him out.)

Our uniqueness is the source of the Life-Work Vocation Questions: *Lord, how am I created in your image? What is the unique conglomeration of gifts, talents, capacities and charisms that is me? How have you formed me in your image, and how are you calling me to participate in your ongoing creation?*

Here we can know the beginnings of the vocation of stewardship, for we are each a steward of our being: heart, mind, soul and strength. Our being is a gift from God, and everything we have, everything we are, everything we will have and will be, everything period, everything belongs to God. For the Bible tells us so:

> *The land shall not be sold irrevocably;*
> *for the land is mine,*
> *and you are but resident aliens*
> *and under my authority.* Leviticus 25:23
>
> *Look, the heavens,*
> *even the highest heavens,*
> *belong to the LORD, your God,*
> *as well as the earth and everything on it.**
>
> Deuteronomy 10:14

Twenty-five years ago now, the U.S. Bishops described stewardship as *a way of life:***

> *Mature disciples make a conscious, firm decision, carried out in action, to be followers of Jesus Christ no matter the cost to themselves.*
>
> *Beginning in conversion, change of mind and heart, this commitment is expressed not in a single action, nor even in a number of actions over a period of time, but in **an entire way of life**. It means committing one's very self to the Lord.*

* See also *God's Money*, Stephen Joseph Wolf, idjc press, 2009.
** *Stewardship: A Disciple's Response*, U.S. Bishops, 1992

Stewardship is an expression of discipleship, with the power to change how we understand and live out our lives. Disciples who practice stewardship recognize God as the origin of life, the giver of freedom, the source of all they have and are and will be.

They are deeply aware of the truth that
"The Lord's are the earth and its fullness;
 the world and those who dwell in it." Ps 24:1

They know themselves to be recipients and caretakers of God's many gifts.

They are grateful for what they have received and eager to cultivate their gifts out of love for God and one another.

To be clear I share this reflection not to suck up to the Bishops, but having prayed with it over the years aware that I could not say it better myself!

Stewardship is about the details of human life and God is in those details. I am also inspired by Kathleen Norris' *The Quotidian Mysteries: Laundry, Liturgy, and "Women's Work"* where she paints this picture for all women and men: Every detail of our life, from folding laundry to paying our bills, can be rituals of discipleship and worship, for we are called to be *good stewards of God's varied grace.* 1 Peter 4:10

Again, this is why we celebrate the feast of *Christ the King*. It is one of the newer feasts in the long history of the Church, and it arose at a time when nationalism was on the rise. We have already seen how *Christ the King* is helpful to the *soldier prophet*. But it is equally important to the *footwasher king* and the *footwasher queen*.

With **royalty** goes privilege, but before that **power!** Every human person is a king, a queen, on for some garden of God's creation, given by God power to do good and to avoid evil, to build justice and to seek peace. Each of us has some power some of the time. Every one of us is a royal power, but we are **vassal** kings and queens. God is the **King** of kings and queens.

What a celebratory feast it can be when a child of God comes to know his or her royal power and surrenders freely the need to be King of kings! It is a grace, a pure gift, to receive the honest capacity to know it and say it: *God is God and I am not*.

By his obedience unto death, Christ communicated to his disciples the gift of **royal freedom**, *so that they might 'by the self-abnegation of a holy life, overcome the reign of sin in themselves.'*   LUMEN GENTIUM 36
Jesus shows us the way to this royal freedom. The saints identify freedom as the capacity to say *Yes*

and only *Yes* to God. When *Yes* finally becomes the only response I can make to God's call, then will I be free in the way the saints understand freedom, for I will no longer be enslaved by any desire that is contrary to my deepest desire, my desire for God. I will only be able to love. So, when will THAT happen? I am still waiting.

Not to overload the topic with tough words of the holy ones, Saint Ignatius of Loyola also offers a pertinent meditation from his *Spiritual Exercises* (#23) called **The Principle and Foundation**:

A. God's Love for you and for me is complete and our God is calling us.

B. Each person is created to praise, revere, and serve our Lord God, and in this vocation to find salvation in eternal life.

C. The other things on the face of the earth are created for us all, to help each person find and fulfill the *purpose/reason/end/...* for which he or she is created.

D. We humans are to use well the other things to the extent they help us discover and fulfill our *purpose/reason/end/...*

E. Sooner or later each of us will need to rid ourselves of the other things that get in the way of this personal vocation.

F. It will come to be our desire to be indifferent to all created things, as far as we are allowed

free choice and consistent with faithful
commitments already freely made.

G. And so, our concern will be to see all good
things in unbiased balance, and we will not
prefer health to sickness, riches to poverty,
the world's honor to its dishonor,
or a long life to a short life, and this balance
of indifference will hold for all other things.

H. When my one desire comes to be
whatever is more conducive to the
purpose/reason/end/... for which I am created,
may my choices reflect that desire.

I. If not now, when?

The letters A-I are added to assist in any discussions.

The shadows of a Royal are the Weakling and the Tyrant. The Weakling may be afraid of power, or may have been kept from discovering his or her giftedness. The Tyrant loves power but for the wrong reasons. What is the right reason? Jesus answers: to wash somebody's feet, to serve. Jesus washed the feet of his own disciples, taking the humble servant's role, giving them a *model* to follow, adding,

If you understand this, blessed are you if you do it.

John 13:16

On the next page is a poem from an Ignatian retreat, an image of myself as the servant whose job Jesus was doing at the footwashing:

Servant at the Last Supper

Lord, I am the servant.
This is my job and it is embarrassing
because I did a job not good enough.
In my hurry, there is still dirt on their feet.
So still serving am I,
an altar boy on Holy Thursday,
helping with basin and towel.
You know the inadequacy on my mind
and smile the way friends do
and assure me with thanks for helping
but that this is not about me.
When you finish with the twelve
you set the basin before me
and taking my feet, one at a time,
wash them completely clean.
Your teaching is a rubbing of word into feet…

I don't hear a word of your teaching,
though I see you talking, them listening,
and John taking it in with good memory.
I trust he'll fill me in later,
but do hear the words I carry always:
> *If you understand this,*
> *blessed are you if you do it.*

Holding the new-clean foot of your servant
you stop talking and enter my eyes
and our tears flow.
You call me messenger.

The child-like spirituality of the royal begins with *freedom from fear and crippling anxieties*, growing up with food, clothing, shelter and love, with an early life free of want and the capacity to trust God and the goodness of people. St. Leo the Great

The good royal comes to decent awareness of his or her gifts and power, and uses them in service of all children of God as a willing footwasher. The *footwasher royal* enters the mystery that in his or her weakness there is also strength.

(2 Corinthians 12:10)

All kings and queens of earth will die, but that is not to be the end of their stories.

QUESTIONS FOR CONSIDERATION

1. What does it mean for me to say that everything belongs to God?

2. How can tithing and other charitable giving be a prayer of gratitude?

3. Lord, show me how you have created me in your image and how you are calling me to grow into the likeness of the Risen Christ.

4. Of which natural talents, gifts, learned skills, and charisms am I aware?

5. Lord, with what garden of creation are you entrusting me?

6. Mrs. Elizabeth Miller, now gone to heaven, often quoted her father who advised her, *Work hard! And pray to Saint Joseph!* What do I think her father meant by that advice?

7. What is the *Quotidian* (everyday ordinary) way I most often pray in a mysterious way?

8. What may sometimes keep me from washing feet?

9. Ponder whether one of these is surfacing:
   - a seed planted
   - a question raised
   - a memory provoked
   - an action prompted

Allow a minute for silent pondering, and then the group may discuss the ponderings (restraining any urge to *fix* anybody).

When time is up:

CLOSING PRAYER
BLESSING VICTIMS OF ADDICTION & VIOLENCE

LEADER

Let us ponder for one minute the Good Samaritan of Luke 10:25-37, who simply responded to the opportunity in front of him to do good.

AFTER A MINUTE OF SILENCE, GROUP MEMBERS TAKE TURNS READING THE INTERCESSIONS

For those addicted to alcohol and drugs,
may God be their strength and their hope:
> ALL *Protect us, Lord, and keep us safe.*

For families and friends of addicts, may they
persevere with love, faith, patience and prudence:
> ALL *Protect us, Lord, and keep us safe.*

For all who are victims of crime or oppression,
we pray that violence may be ceased everywhere:
> ALL *Protect us, Lord, and keep us safe.*

For those who harm others, may they turn to God
for the grace of conversion and new life:
> ALL *Protect us, Lord, and keep us safe.*

ALL **God of mercy, look with compassion on all who have lost health and freedom to addiction. Restore to them the assurance of your mercy and strengthen them in the work of recovery. Relieve the suffering of victims of violence; grant them peace of mind, a renewed faith, and trust in your protection and care. Protect us all from violence, keep us safe from weapons of hate, and restore to us the tranquility of true peace.   Our Father . . .**

EPHESIANS 1 — GOD's ONEs
Melody: *Joyful, Joyful, We Adore Thee*

Bless-ed be the God and Fa-ther
of our Lord/ Je-sus Christ,
who has blessed us in the Christ\,
bless-ings in their Spir-it breath.
As God chose us in the Mes-si-ah
be-fore/ found-ing sky or earth,
to be ho-ly, clean of blem-ish,
in God's eye: a-dop-tion worth.

In the Son we have re-demp-tion,
God's for-give-ness of our sin,
by the rich-es of his grace\
lav-ished on us gath-ered in.
Giv-ing wis-dom, know-ledge/, vis-ion,
mys-t'ry/ of the Fa-ther's will,
sum-ming up all things in Je-sus,
fa-vored in the full-ness sent.

In our hear-ing of the gos-pel
word of our sal-va\-tion,
one by one we too were cho-sen,
joined as part-ners with the Son.
By the prom-is'd Ho-ly/ Spir-it,
signed and/ sealed as heirs of God,
God's pos-ses-sion, God's re-demp-tion,
God's be-lov-ed, Ab-ba's own.

Text: Ephesians 1:3-14, Stephen J. Wolf, 2008, with gratitude to the Institute for Priestly Formation
Music: 8787D, HYMN TO JOY, Ludwig van Beethoven, d. 1827; adpt. by Edward Hodges, 1824

Beloved Lover

*You are my beloved son/daughter;
in you I take great delight!*

☐ SONG (from page 66), all together

Keeping a finger on this page, go to PAGE 15
and take turns reading down the *Beloved Lover* column.

A member of the group reads **1st Corinthians 13:1-13**
while others read along in their Bibles.   *(Love is…)*

A member of the group reads **John 15:1-17**
while others read along in their Bibles.   *(Vine & Branches)*

LEADER And we read in the book of Wisdom,

8:2,3,21;9:4a

*Her I loved and sought after from my youth;
I sought to take her for my bride
and was enamored of her beauty.
She adds to nobility
the splendor of companionship with God;
even the Ruler of all loved her.
And knowing that I could not otherwise possess her
unless God gave it - and this, too was prudence,
to know whose gift she is -*

I went to the Lord and besought him,
and said with all my heart…
Give me Wisdom…

The word of the Lord.   ALL   **Thanks be to God**

Then group members take turns reading the following:

Having created us in God's own image, God has created within us a longing, a yearning, a *capacity* for God. I hear people calling this sacred space in us the *God hole*. This is part of what it is to be a human person, for no human being is created without it. Every honest and true desire of a human being is some reflection of our deepest desire, which is our desire for God.

Ever think of the *Catechism* as poetry?

> **The desire for God**
> **is written in the human heart,**
> **because the human person**
> **is created by God and for God;**
> **and God never ceases to draw**
> **the human being to God's own self.**
>
> **Only in God will the human person**
> **find the truth and happiness**
> **for which we never stop searching.**

see CCC 27

Part of the Christian journey is to let this into the bones of one's being, or rather, to recognize, to know newly, this truth as already part of our being.

In his 1948 best selling autobiography *The Seven Storey Mountain*, Thomas Merton tells how in his mid-twenties he was guided to this truth by his close friend, Robert Lax, who helped his friend see the deepest desire of Merton's heart, to be a saint. Merton first rejected sainthood as plainly impossible for him, so Lax continued with this question for all vocations:

> *Don't you believe*
> *that God will make you*
> *what God created you to be,*
> *if you will consent to let God do it?*
> *All you have to do is desire it.*

Decades later in *New Seeds of Contemplation* one of the Trappist monk's many descriptions of prayer would be God speaking God's name in the center of our soul.

There is a tradition about Saint John the Evangelist, the tradition of the Beloved Disciple of Jesus, that people kept coming to him in his old age for more insight and knowledge, for more of his witness-testimony about Jesus, and that he would simply tell them over and over, *Little children, love one another.*

This is our vocation, to love one another. The word *vocation* is from the Latin *vocare* (hear *voice* and *vocal*) meaning *calling*. This call comes to each of us all through our lives in many and varied ways, and God is the One doing the calling. This is the source of the love-life vocation question for every *beloved lover* baptized follower of Jesus the Christ:

> *Lord, you know me.*
> *You know everything about me.*
> *You know me better than I know myself.*
> *Please come forth now*
>   *with some of what you know.*
> *What is it, Lord?*
> *What is the form of life*
>   *into which you are calling me*
>   *that I might best and most fully*
>   *love and be loved?*
> *Is it the sacrament of marriage?*
> *Is it as a generous single person?*
> *Is it religious life or ordination?*
> *Speak, Lord, so that I may hear your call;*
> *help me, Lord, so that I may say my Yes.*

Let me share some advice of Teri Bosio from her own vocation calling into marriage, who I first came to know as a Director of Religious Education, and which I often pass on to young adults:

*If you think that God is going to be calling you
into the sacrament of marriage,
ask God, beginning this day,
and every day until and into your marriage,
ask God, who already knows who you will marry,
to watch over that person.*

May I also encourage all parents, grandparents, godparents, teachers, coaches, aunts and uncles to pass on Teri's counsel.

Intercessory prayer is the riskiest form of prayer. If I keep asking God to feed God's hungry people, God might respond to my prayer by sending me to do the feeding. If I keep asking God to watch over the person with whom I will someday live in the sacrament of marriage, if God is going to answer that prayer, then the way that I too live for the rest of my life will be part of God's answer. If God is going to watch over my future spouse, God is going to be prompting me to grow into the man or woman God created me to be. God will be prompting me to do good and avoid evil. Might this even affect how I date and how I grow in the capacity for friendship and heart-to-heart human intimacy in every relationship?

If you are already married, praying for your spouse will of necessity have some impact on how you live now in the day-to-day stuff of the covenant of marriage. Your marriage is a symbol *for* all of God's people of the covenant that God has made *with* all of God's people, and God has promised us that God will always be faithful in that covenant. As the shortest of the 150 psalms sings plainly, *the Lord is faithful forever.*   Psalm 117:2

If you sense that God is calling you into the generous single vocation, let me prepare you for awareness that the world will try to tell you that you are a failure as a human being if you are uncoupled. The best response I know to this message of our culture is, excuse me, *bull----*. Don't mind you quoting me on this one.

I agree with Debra Farrington in *One Like Jesus*:

> *Nowhere in the bible does it say that*
> *God loves us better when we are married.*
> *We are not incomplete halves that God*
> *will love better when made whole...*

The world has always been in great need of healthy and generous men and women who can discern and celebrate the call to the single life. Parents are overwhelmed. Aunts, uncles, cousins, big brothers and sisters, neighbors, teachers, coaches, catechists, all around us are young folks who are looking for faith mentors on the journey of life. There are also uncountable ways God calls single folks to heroic work with God's poor and marginalized and elders in need of companions, and as missionaries. The generous single vocation can help allow the freedom needed to respond to these needs.

In *The Joy of Love* (*para. 158*) Pope Francis quotes the 2015 Synod of Bishops, adding to the short sentences in the *Catechism* (*see page 5*) about the generous single vocation:

> *Many people who are unmarried are not only devoted to their own family but often render great service in their group of friends, in the Church community, and in their professional lives. Sometimes their presence and contributions are overlooked causing in them a sense of isolation. Many put their talents at the service of the Christian community through charity and volunteer work. Others remain unmarried because they consecrate their lives to the love of Christ and neighbor. Their dedication greatly enriches the family, the Church, and society.*

Here is a challenge for our Church: How can we better celebrate the generous single vocation? I wonder how many marriages happen out of the desire to be seen as a successful or normal human being. I wonder how many divorced single adults have discerned God's call to the generous single vocation by way of marriage and divorce. How many divorces are rooted in cultural pressure to be coupled?

Perhaps the anniversary of the sacrament of Baptism or of Confirmation would be a good day to celebrate one's generous single vocation. Another opportunity might be the Vigil of Pentecost or that Sunday night, again giving honor to the sacrament of Confirmation as the sacrament of vocation for those in the single life. A married woman complained about this suggestion, for she said Pentecost is her feast too. But I don't hear a contra complaint on Mothers Day or when we bless marriages near Valentine's Day.

I searched in vain for a universally recognized patron saint of the single vocation. They surface in primarily adverse circumstances. For that matter, even in the year 2015, the Synod of Bishops could not bring itself to use the word *single*, using the word *unmarried*. Some folks have even suggested that the single life is not a vocation but a lack of a vocation. Would this likewise suggest that celibacy is not a true *charism* but some kind of deficiency?

Lifting up the generous single vocation is in no way a slam against marriage. In a conference to some nuns in Kentucky, Thomas Merton said, *modern married life is complicated and rough and it's a lot simpler to be celibate. But when two people are very much in love with each other, this business of carrying one another's burdens is immensely simplified. Of course, it wears off and gets rough again.*

Springs of Contemplation

There indeed seem to be many in our culture who are resisting the call into the sacrament of Marriage as Pope Francis said, for fear of making a commitment of one's entire life. But not all human beings are or ever have been wired for marriage. To quote Father Bill Fleming again, *Everyone has a right to marriage, but we're not all capable of it*, and he would point to himself and add with a big smile, *Exhibit A!*

In her groundbreaking and timely work on *charisms*, Sherry Anne Weddell discusses *celibacy* as the experience of these as true: *Being single is personally and spiritually very satisfying for me. I enjoy and love others but don't really want to be in a committed romantic relationship. I want to be free to commit myself totally to a particular call or vocation. I identify with the experience of many great Christians who were celibate. Friendship, rather than romance, is the most compelling relationship in my life.*

The Catholic Spiritual Gifts Inventory

May I suggest these five sentences as retreat ponderings for anyone discerning the possible call to the generous single vocation, or for anyone praying for such a person. We will discuss *charisms* more thoroughly in the next chapter.

Besides trusting in God's call to fidelity in prayer, the other best advice I know to give to a man or woman called to the generous single vocation is to attend to friendships, especially to old friendships. Two of the greatest gifts of my life are my gang of friends, some of whom go back to the first grade, and my seven brothers. These are the people who know me, for good and for ill, and who leave me no choice in their presence except to simply be myself.

When I feel disconnected or isolated, one lunch with a brother or one authentic phone call or meal shared with one of this gang of friends, and all is well again. With everyone so busy, gatherings of a whole gang of friends or family can become rare. But they are always banquets, and Christ is always in the room.

When a disciple or a family gets dislocated, moving away from sources of lifelong friends, our Church these days offers a vital source for connection. These are usually called *small group faith sharing communities* or some variation of these words. Faith Sharing Groups will continue to give witness to the presence of the Risen Lord, *where two or three are gathered* in his name.

Matthew 18:20

If your parish does not offer faith sharing groups, consider forming one yourself. Begin with this book, and later consider others at *idjc.org*. Or use some other resource. For some groups it's the Sunday Mass readings. Some use the *Catechism* or choose together a book on Jesus or on prayer. Some groups form after weekend retreats. For some in addiction, a twelve-step group can meet the need. Some parishes have rosary groups or folks gathering for the *Liturgy of the Hours*. Also most religious orders support Lay Associate or Oblate processes.

One chief difference between the generous single vocation and religious life is the question of living alone versus living in community. Neither is better than the other; the question is, *what is your call, your vocation?* For many, the first question for religious life is the calling or *charism* of the particular order, generally some reflection of the witness of the founder of the religious order.

If it feels as if this chapter leans toward the single vocation, you are correct. But in a similarly organized little book, *Being Spouses*, I begin with this official definition:

> *The matrimonial covenant by which a man and a woman establish between themselves a partnership of the whole of life, is by its nature ordered toward the good of the spouses and the procreation and education of offspring; this covenant between baptized persons has been raised by Christ the Lord to the dignity of a sacrament.* CCC 1601

and continue with this parish priest's practical definition of the sacrament of marriage:

> *When a grown-up baptized bride*
> *and a grown-up baptized groom*
> *with a good sense of who they are*
> *reveal themselves to each other*
> *and then come together in freedom*
> *and in freedom exchange mutual consent*
> *to bond in   1. permanence, and*
> *   2. fidelity, and*
> *   3. openness to children.*
>
> *Being Spouses: from Celibate Observation*
> Stephen Joseph Wolf, idjc press, 2009.

Jesus has called us *friends* (John 15:15). And his parting words are *I am with you always* (Matthew 28:20). The disciples became his companions, as he is our companion. The friendship relationship with Jesus often happens in the teen years. But many adults somehow missed it or have no memory of it, and later discover the desire to develop this friendship. It is a beautiful thing.

But long before Jesus called us friends, or promised to be with us always, he experienced the complete and overwhelming love of his Abba when being baptized in the Jordan River, hearing the truth: *You are my beloved Son, with you I am well pleased* (Mark 1:11; Luke 3:22). In Matthew, the words are addressed to the witnesses, and so also to us: *This is my beloved Son, with whom I am well pleased.* Perhaps both happened, so that Jesus could know it in his humanity and so could those witnesses. To desire to be loved is one kind of blessing. To know you *are* is quite another.

Shadows of the Lover are Addiction and Impotence. The Addict chases after pleasure until he or she is no longer free. The one who has not been taught love can be trapped in impotence of the heart, outside Christ's intimate desire for us, that we *might have life and to the full* (John 10:10), the loving way of the Beloved Son of God.

The child-like spirituality of the lover begins with *sociability, getting along with others*, where the image of God in everyone can train us to avoid prejudice and be at peace with our nature as social beings.
St. Leo the Great

To circle back, we can make perhaps a tortuous distinction between being a minister and being an apostle. An **apostle** is *one who is sent*. Sent out. A **minister** is *one who serves*. Ministers do often serve outside the community of believers, but we usually think of ministry as something that happens within a community, as when a parent tends to, ministers to, a sick child. Apostles do often give witness to the Risen Lord within a community, but we usually think of the apostolate as something that happens outside the community, when one is sent into the world or to the marketplace. A helpful if tortured distinction.

So think here of a *footwasher royal* as one who witnesses to the resurrection of Jesus Christ by doing good works in the community at large, staying ready to speak a word about Jesus. In this sense, a *footwasher royal* is primarily but not solely an *apostle*.

But a *beloved lover* as one who knows so well that he or she is loved completely by God that no loving task in the community is too small.

QUESTIONS FOR CONSIDERATION

1. A wise fella once said,
   Intimacy is a basic human need; we find a healthy way to tend to it, or it will tend to us.
   One definition of *intimacy* is to be graced with time with someone who truly knows me, the grace of knowing and being known.
   Do I have a better way to say this?

2. We call it providence
   when at a wedding we are able to say,
   Thank God for getting those two together!
   What role has providence played in my life?

3. According to *Retrouvaille*, one of the good ministries to married couples, the four stages in a mature marriage are
   (1) Romance,   (3) Misery
   (2) Disillusionment (4) Awakening.
   At first glance how do these seem to me?

4. What advice would I give my godchild about marriage or the single vocation?

5. As Jesus knew himself to be a Beloved Lover, am I growing into a more loving person?

6. How might I encourage a neighbor who is single?

7. If the pope came to our parish and
   asked us to call one priest into holy orders
   and one sister into religious life,
   who would I invite into discernment?

8. It seems to happen that when I remember
   having sinned, in that moment I was not in
   a state of awareness of God's complete love
   for me. How might I stay in this awareness?

9. Can I imagine a liturgical ritual where
   a parishioner could publicly embrace
   the generous single vocation?
   What would it look like?

10. Ponder whether one of these is surfacing:
    - a seed planted   - a question raised
    - a memory provoked - an action prompted

Allow a minute for silent pondering, and then the group may discuss the ponderings (restraining any urge to *fix* anybody).

When time is up:
                    CLOSING PRAYER
                    BLESSING FAMILIES

LEADER   **The grace of our Lord Jesus Christ
           be with us all, now and forever.**

*AFTER ONE MORE MINUTE OF SILENCE,
GROUP MEMBERS TAKE TURNS
READING THE INTERCESSIONS*

Lord Jesus, you consecrated the domestic church
through your obedience to Mary and Joseph:
>   ALL   *Lord, keep families in your peace.*

Your heart was set on the concerns of your Abba;
may every home be a place of reverence:
>   ALL   *Lord, keep families in your peace.*

You loved and were loved by your friends;
help all households to remain in your love:
>   ALL   *Lord, keep families in your peace.*

At the beginning of a new family in Cana you
changed water into wine in your miraculous sign:
>   ALL   *Lord, keep families in your peace.*

You lived the ultimate generous single vocation
and a new archetype of the religious vocation;
may all singles and religious know themselves
always as members of the one family of God:
>   ALL   *Lord, keep families in your peace.*

ALL   **We bless your name, O Lord, for sending your incarnate Son as part of a family, that living its life he would know its worries and joys. Watch over all extended families; may they bear witness as domestic churches to your glory.**

Our Father . . .

O/ breathe on me, O/ breath of God,
Fill/ me with life a//-new,
That I may love what you have loved,
And do what you would do.

O/ breathe on me, O/ breath of God,
Un/-til my heart is// pure,
Un-til with you I will one will,
To do and to en-dure.

O/ breathe on me, O/ breath of God,
In/-spire my bu-sy// mind,
Un-til this earth-ly part of me
Glows with your fire div-ine.

O/ breathe on me, O/ breath of God,
My/ soul shall nev-er// die,
But live in your e-ter-nal life,
Your love the rea-son why.

Text: Edwin Hatch, 1878, altered
Music: ST. COLUMBA, CM; Gaelic Folk Melody
Melody: *The King Of Love My Shepherd Is*

Vocation Gifted

*I have come
that they may have life
and to the full.* John 10:10

☐ SONG (from page 84), all together

Keeping a finger on this page, go to PAGE 15
and take a minute to review all four columns.

LEADER: Before we hear the scripture readings, a confession from the author: The more accurate title for this chapter would be **Charisms**, but that word spooks many Catholics. Don't run out of the room yet! First, at least listen to passages of letters from the tradition of Saint Paul and a couple of paragraphs from the *Catechism*:

A member of the group reads **1st Corinthians 12:4-31a**
while others read along in their Bibles: (see below)

READER: A reading from the First Letter
of Saint Paul to the Corinthians: 12:4-31a

There are different kinds of spiritual gifts (*charismata*) but the same Spirit; there are different forms of service (*diakonia*) but the same Lord; there are different workings (*energemata*) but the same God who produces all of them in everyone. To each individual the manifestation of the Spirit is given for some benefit (*sumpheron*, "the common good"). To one is given through the Spirit the expression of <u>wisdom</u>; to another the expression of <u>knowledge</u> according to the same Spirit; to another <u>faith</u> by the same Spirit; to another gifts of <u>healing</u> by the one Spirit; to another <u>mighty deeds</u>; to another <u>prophecy</u>; to another <u>discernment of spirits</u>; to another varieties of <u>tongues</u>; to another <u>interpretation of tongues</u>. But one and the same Spirit produces all of these, distributing them individually to each person as he wishes.

As a body is one though it has many parts (*melos*, "members"), and all the parts of the body, though many, are one body, so also Christ. For in one Spirit we were all baptized into one body, whether Jews or Greeks, slaves or free persons, and we were all given to drink of one Spirit.

Now the body is not a single part, but many. If a foot should say, "Because I am not a hand I do not belong to the body," it does not for this reason belong any less to the body. Or if an ear should say, "Because I am not an eye I do not belong to the body," it does not for this reason belong any less to the body. If the whole body were an eye, where would the hearing be? If the whole body were hearing where would the sense of smell be? But as it is, God placed the parts, each one of them, in the body as he intended. If they were all one part, where would the body be? But as it is there are many parts, yet one body. The eye cannot say to the hand, "I do not need you," nor again the head to the feet, "I do not need you." Indeed, the parts of the body that seem to be weaker are all the more necessary, and those parts of the body that we consider less honorable we surround with greater honor, and our less presentable parts are treated with greater propriety, whereas our more presentable parts do not need this. But God has so constructed the body as to give greater honor to a part that is without it, so that there may be no division in the body, but that the parts may have the same concern for one another. If one part suffers, all the parts suffer with it; if one part is honored, all the parts share its joy.

Now you are Christ's body, and individually parts of it. Some people God has designated in the church to be first, <u>apostles</u>; second, <u>prophets</u>; third, <u>teachers</u>; then <u>mighty deeds</u>; then, gifts (*charismata*) of <u>healing</u>, <u>assistance</u>, <u>administration</u>, and varieties of <u>tongues</u>. Are all apostles? Are all prophets? Are all teachers? Do all work mighty deeds? Do all have gifts of healing? Do all speak in tongues? Do all interpret? Strive eagerly for the greatest <u>spiritual gifts</u> (*charismata*).

But I shall show you a still more excellent way.

The word of the Lord.   ALL   **Thanks be to God**

> Saint Paul's *still more excellent way? faith, hope and love,...but the greatest of these is love.*   1st Cor 13:13

A member of the group reads **Romans 12:1-8**
while others read along in their Bibles: (see below)

READER: A reading from the Letter
of Saint Paul to the Romans: 12:1-8

I urge you therefore, brothers and sisters, by the mercies of God, to offer your bodies as a living sacrifice, holy and pleasing to God, your spiritual worship. Do not conform yourselves to this age but be transformed by the renewal of your mind, that you may discern what is the will of God, what is good and pleasing and perfect.

For by the grace (*charis*) given to me I tell everyone among you not to think of yourself more highly than one ought to think, but to think soberly, each according to the measure of faith that God has apportioned. For as in one body we have many parts and all the parts do not have the same function (*praxin*), so we, though many, are one body in Christ and individually parts of one another. Since we have gifts (*charismata*) that differ according to the grace (*charis*) given to us, let us exercise them: if prophecy, in proportion to the faith; if ministry, in the ministering (*diakonia*, "service"); if one is a teacher, in teaching; if one exhorts, in exhortation (*paraklesis*, "encouragement"); if one contributes, in generosity; if one is over others ("governing"), with diligence; if one does acts of mercy, with cheerfulness.

The word of the Lord.   ALL   ***Thanks be to God***

VOCATION GIFTED

A member of the group reads **Ephesians 4:7, 11-16**
while others read along in their Bibles: (see below)

READER: A reading from
the Letter to the Ephesians: 4:7,11-16

But grace (*charis*) was given to each of us according to the measure of Christ's gift…

And he gave some as <u>apostles</u>, others as <u>prophets</u>, others as <u>evangelists</u>, others as <u>pastors</u> (*poimenas*, "shepherds") and <u>teachers</u>, to equip the holy ones for the work of ministry (*diakonia*), for building up the body of Christ, until we all attain to the unity of faith and knowledge of the Son of God, to mature manhood (*andra teleion*, "a human of complete maturity"), to the extent of the full share of Christ, so that we may no longer be infants, tossed by waves and swept along by every wind of teaching arising from human trickery, from their cunning in the interests of scheming. Rather, living the truth in love, we should grow in every way into him who is the head, Christ, from whom the whole body, joined and held together by every supporting ligament, with the proper functioning of each part, brings about the body's growth and builds itself up in love (*agape*).

The word of the Lord.   ALL   **Thanks be to God**

ONE MINUTE OF SILENCE

Then group members take turns reading the following:

Grace is first and foremost the gift of the Spirit who justifies and sanctifies us. But grace also includes the gifts that the Spirit grants us to associate us with the work of the Spirit, to enable us to collaborate in the salvation of others and in the growth of the Body of Christ, the Church. These are *sacramental graces*, gifts proper to the different sacraments. There are furthermore *special graces*, also called *charisms* after the Greek term used by St. Paul and meaning "favor," "gratuitous gift," "benefit" (Cf. LG 12). Whatever their character -- sometimes it is extraordinary, such as the gift of miracles or of tongues -- charisms are oriented toward sanctifying grace and are intended for the common good of the Church. They are at the service of charity which builds up the Church. (Cf. 1 Cor 12)   *Catechism of the Catholic Church* CCC 2003

Whether extraordinary or simple or humble, charisms are graces of the Holy Spirit which directly or indirectly benefit the Church, ordered as they are to her **building up**, to the **good of human beings**, and to the **needs of the world**. CCC 799

Charisms are to be accepted with **gratitude** by the person who receives them and by all members of the Church as well. They are a wonderfully rich grace for the apostolic vitality and for the holiness of the entire Body of Christ, provided they really are genuine gifts of the Holy Spirit and are used in full conformity with authentic promptings of this same Spirit, that is, in keeping with **charity**, the true measure of all charisms. (Cf. 1 Corinthians 13)   CCC 800

It is in this sense that **discernment** of charisms is always necessary. No charism is exempt from being referred and submitted to the Church's shepherds. "Their office [is] not indeed to extinguish the Spirit, but to test all things and hold fast to what is good," (LG12; cf.30; *1Thess5:12,19-21*; John Paul II, *Christifidelis Laici*,24) so that all the diverse and complementary charisms work together **"for the common good"** (1 Corinth. 12:7).
Catechism of the Catholic Church CCC 801

A very important acknowledgement is necessary before going any further. Without the work of Sherry Anne Weddell, Fr. Michael Sweeney, O.P., and all the good folks of *The Catherine of Siena Institute*, and their support from the West Coast Dominicans, I would know little about ***charisms***. Their study gives us the 23 Common Charisms listed on page 93. The very next time you are on what my Dad used to call *the ultra-net*, visit **www. siena.org**. Find one of their *Called and Gifted Workshops* and travel to it. With gratitude, here is an attempt at defining a ***charism***:

> A grace-gift given by God, Father and Son, through their Breath we call the Holy Spirit, into a Confirmed Christian that empowers us to accomplish good things desired by God for the common good and for building up the body of Christ in ways that are beyond our natural talents and abilities and capacities but not beyond the design and power of God.

Signs that a confirmed Christian is using a ***charism*** are:

(**A**) a life-giving sense of the peaceful energy of being in God's flow,
(**B**) unusually effective results in using the gift,
(**C**) direct or indirect feedback from others, and
(**D**) that the gift is always used for others.

After fourteen tax seasons as an accountant, my thinking tends to rows and columns. So the chart on the next page is one way to see *charisms* in relation to other ways that God gifts us:

We are created in the image of God, and the *Imago Dei* cannot be taken from us. Every human is given some measure of the Human or Moral Virtues: *Prudence* (using reason to choose the good), *Fortitude* (strength in difficulties), *Justice* (firm will to give God and neighbor their due); and *Temperance* (moderating balance in the use of created goods). As with an athlete's muscles, we grow in their use, or not as they atrophy.

In Baptism we enter a more intimate relationship with the Holy Spirit, who guides us with *Faith*, *Hope*, and *Love*. We also receive the seven *Sanctifying Gifts* of the Holy Spirit.

In the sacrament of Confirmation, the Church tells us, we then receive the fullness of the Gifts of the Holy Spirit, all seven of which are given to us so that we can be most fully ourselves, and to use for the good of others.

In addition to all this, **Charisms** are given to us as supernatural gifts, enabling us to do the good in ways beyond our nature. Each Christian is given at least one permanent lifelong *charism*, to most more. Only Jesus has received them all.

VOCATION GIFTED

FOUR HUMAN VIRTUES	THREE THEOLOGICAL VIRTUES	SEVEN GIFTS OF THE HOLY SPIRIT	TWENTY-THREE COMMON CHARISMS
			Administration
		Wisdom	Celibacy
Prudence			Craftsmanship
			Encouragement
		Understanding	Evangelism
	Faith		Extraordinary Faith
			Giving
		Counsel	Healing
Fortitude			Helps
			Hospitality
		Fortitude	Intercessory prayer
	Hope		Knowledge
			Leadership
		Knowledge	Mercy
Justice			Missionary
			Music
		Piety	Pastoring
	Charity (Love)		Prophecy
			Service
		Fear of the Lord	Teaching
Temperance			Voluntary poverty
			Wisdom
			Writing
			more?

CREATION	BAPTISM	CONFIRMATION	CHRISTIAN LIFE
Talents & Virtues *Use 'em or lose 'em.*	Now in a relationship with the Holy Spirit	Sanctifying Gifts for self **and** for others	Charisms are **always** for the benefit of others.

ORGANIZATION - **So Good Things Can Happen**
  Administration   planning, coordination, delegation
  Leadership   sharing a compelling vision with buy-in
  Service   see & actively fill gaps & unmet needs
  Giving   cheerful generosity to meet unmet needs

UNDERSTANDING - **The Ways of Creation, Humanity, & God**
  Knowledge   study & learning for its own sake
  Wisdom   insight that leads to creative solutions

CREATIVITY - **Toward Order & Beauty**
  Craftsmanship   creative work with physical materials
  Writing   words for truth, beauty, & glory to God
  Music   for the delight of others or praise of God

COMMUNICATION - **Truth that Transforms**
  Teaching   skills & information for human potential
  Evangelism   drawing others into Jesus' discipleship
  Prophecy   message(s) God wants heard

PASTORING - **For Nurture of People**
  Encouragement   through presence and words of comfort
  Helps   enabling others to use their gifts
  Mercy   practical deeds to relieve suffering
  Hospitality   welcoming with food, shelter, friendship
  Pastoring   long-term spiritual growth of a group

HEALING - **When Healing Is Otherwise Unlikely**
  Intercessory prayer   God's love and care for others
  Healing   a way God cures, usually by touch

LIFESTYLE - **Freedom for Unusual Ministry**
  Extraordinary Faith   exceptional trust & freedom to act
  Voluntary poverty   cheerful simplicity with the poor
  Missionary   using charisms in another culture
  Celibacy   fruitfully unmarried for Christ

To repeat, every Confirmed Catholic has received one or more (but not all) of the common *charisms*. To be sure, there are many more, but these are the ones that seem to show themselves in most parish communities.

It is also common for someone to have a mix of two or more *charisms*, where one assists another. For example, someone with the *charism* of teaching might also have the gift of knowledge.

No one but God can tell any of us that we have a *charism*. However, it is good for all of us to be familiar with all of them, so that when we think we see a *charism* being used by someone we can tell them something like, *Hey Joe, it looks to me as if you might have the **charism** of craftsmanship*. This is called *direct feedback*. In contrast, *indirect feedback* can be when people keep asking me to do things that involve using the gift.

A *Called and Gifted Workshop* gives a disciple the chance to hear about the *charisms* and to take **The Catholic Spiritual Gifts Inventory**. The inventory is not designed to tell you what your *charisms* are, but to give you clues so that you can begin discernment.

The root meaning of discernment is *to cut away* everything that is not the thing for which we are looking. It can be a very fruitful spirituality or lifelong way to keep listening to how God keeps trying to use us in the world and in the Church.

Let me share a frustration that I have felt as a pastor. The bulk of the good things that are being done by God through the Church does not happen on our parish campuses, but rather in the markets, offices, schools, workplaces, shops, and neighborhoods where Christians are sent by God each week at the end of Sunday Mass.

For sure there are good things happening in every parish. But those are done by ministers who are there to support the real work of the Church by all the apostles-in-the-world. I find myself a bit frustrated because parishioners do not believe me when I tell them that knowing about *charisms* is in the first place **not** about recruiting parish volunteers.

The next time you are at Sunday Mass, count the number of people who are ministers in the assembly. *Everybody else there* is an apostle about to be sent as the presence of Christ the Risen Lord to the broader community, especially to those places no priest or deacon or sister could even get to. When I was a CPA, often did I field curious workplace questions about the Catholic faith. As a parish priest, almost all of my time is spent with other Catholics.

Does it frighten you to think of yourself as an apostle? Aren't the Bishops the successors to the apostles? So are you. *For the bible tells me so...*

In the first chapter of the Book of Acts, sometimes called the Acts of the Apostles, Jesus had ascended to the Father. While waiting for the coming of the Holy Spirit, the "eleven" decided to choose someone to take the place of Judas Iscariot, the betrayer. Simon says,

> *Therefore, it is necessary that one*
> *of those who accompanied us the whole time*
> *the Lord Jesus came and went among us,*
> *beginning from the baptism of John until*
> *the day on which he was taken up from us,*
> *become with us a witness to his resurrection.*
> Acts 1:21-22

Think you could stand up in front of ten people and tell the story of the baptism of Jesus? Sure you could! Think you could stand up in front of ten people and tell about Jesus' three years of teaching and preaching and healing? For sure you can talk about the parts that have made all the difference to you! Think you could stand up in front of ten people and tell the story of the crucifixion of Jesus? Yeah, we Catholics have that one down! Think you could stand up in front of ten people and tell the story of the resurrection appearances and the ascension? Sure you could! Congratultions! You have a *masters* in being an apostle! Perhaps you want to say, *But I was not there!* Well, you might as well have been.

In the late 1940's high-schooler Charlie was working at a gas station two houses down from where Jeanette Gregory's family lived. She had a thing for Charlie, and when he was behind the gas station fixing a flat tire, she would figure out a way to be in the back yard. Charlie and Jeanette would have eight sons. I am number two.

Was I there? Not really; but I might as well have been, for that story is so much a part of my story that without it I would not even be.

The story of the baptism, ministry, death and resurrection of Jesus the Christ is so much a part of your story that you might as well have been there. By the way, the same is true of the Hebrew scriptures: They were in Jesus, so they are part of the life story of every Christian.

Notice too that Simon Peter gives us a kind of job title: **Witness to the Resurrection.** Indeed, we receive on Sunday and carry into the world for each week the real presence of Jesus Christ, the Risen Lord. Everything we do comes out of the life, death, resurrection, and ascension, and the breath of the Holy Spirit of Father and Son.

VOCATION GIFTED

The Church exists to evangelize, to spread the good news to those by whom God wishes it be heard. *Lay faithful find themselves on the front lines of the Church's life (and) ought to have an ever-clearer consciousness not only of belonging to the Church, but of **being** the Church... These are the Church.* Pope Piux XII

Can you see how a Seeker and *Lifegiver Priest* might be assisted in his or her vocation by the charism of extraordinary faith, healing, intercessory prayer, mercy, or wisdom...?

Can you see how a Disciple, a *Soldier Prophet* might be assisted in his or her vocation by the charism of helps, knowledge, missionary, prophecy, teaching, voluntary poverty, or writing...?

Can you see how an Apostle and *Footwasher Royal* might be assisted in his or her vocation by the charism of administration, craftsmanship, evangelism, giving, leadership, or service...?

Can you see how a Minister and *Beloved Lover* might be assisted in his or her vocation by the charism of celibacy, encouragement, hospitality, music, or pastoring...?

You might want to arrange them in a different way that makes more sense to how these four vocations to *Holy Life* (priest), *True Life* (prophet), *Life Work* (royal), and *Love Life* (beloved lover) show up in the life of you.

Is one of the common charisms (or another gift not named on page 94) crossing your mind as a possible charism which God might have given you as a lifelong permanent charism? If so, be not afraid of this exercise: When you get a chance, find a pencil and some paper, offer a prayer for enlightenment from God, and make a list of all the events in your life when that charism might have been active. Note whether the four signs of a charism (at the bottom of page 91) seem to have been present. Then seek out a conversation with a companion or a spiritual director.

What is God up to with you? How is God already using you in the mission of the Son? How are the Father and the Son breathing their Holy Spirit-Breath onto and into you?

If you can know what your natural gifts and talents and capacities are… If you can discover the charism(s) through which God has already been using you… If you can become aware of the way the suffering and brokenness of the world haunts your soul… Where these meet you might discover your vocation wrapped up in all the vocations of Jesus our Christ, priest and prophet and king and beloved, and receive the free grace to join Mary, the Mother of God, in your own

be it done unto me according to your Word.

VOCATION GIFTED

QUESTIONS FOR CONSIDERATION

1. Before our Rite of Welcome in the R.C.I.A. process, we ask catechumens and candidates, *What are you seeking?* So, what am I seeking?

2. Can I name something that Jesus is trying to teach me as his disciple?

3. Am I aware of a truth that God has been preparing me to speak to someone, some group of people, or to the world? Who is a good person with whom I can discuss this?

4. Can I name a time when I have been aware of being an apostle in the world?

5. Describe an event when God seems to have used me for someone else with remarkable results, when I had *an unmistakable inner experience of peace, energy and joy?* Can someone in the group name a charism from page 94 that might have been used?

7. Cardinal Suenens suggested living such that my life would not make sense if God did not exist. Anything keeping me from doing this?

7. Ponder whether one of these is surfacing:
   - a seed planted
   - a question raised
   - a memory provoked
   - an action prompted

When time is up: CLOSING PRAYER
BLESSING PILGRIMS

LEADER The *Canticle of Zechariah,* father of John the
Baptist, is used each day in Morning Prayer:
ALL   Luke 1:68-79

**Blessed be the Lord the God of Israel
who chose a people,
visited them to bring redemption,
and raised salvation in the house of David,
saving strength from God's own servant,
speaking from the age of the prophets
through the mouth of the holy prophet:
Salvation out of enmity,
even out of those who hate us,
to show our ancestors how mercy works,
and to remember the holy promise of the Lord,
the covenant made for our father Abraham,
calming our fear and making us free
to serve God as holy and righteous and just
in the Lord's presence all our days.
And you also child
will be called a prophet of the Most High
for you will go before the Lord to prepare his way
and give to his people a knowledge of salvation
known in accepting forgiveness of their sins.
From the deepness of God's mercy on us,
a sun rising from the height will visit to appear
to those who sit in the dark or shadow of death,
and to guide our feet into the way of peace.**

VOCATION GIFTED

GROUP MEMBERS TAKE TURNS READING THE INTERCESSIONS

Father all-holy, of old you made yourself guide to your people in the desert wandering:
> ALL **Lord, be our companion on this journey.**

You have given us your only begotten Son to be our way to you:
> ALL **Lord, be our companion on this journey.**

You gave us Mary as image and model for following Christ:
> ALL **Lord, be our companion on this journey.**

With your Son, you guide your pilgrim Church on earth through the Holy Spirit:
> ALL **Lord, be our companion on this journey.**

Grant that we may one day see you face to face:
> ALL **Lord, be our companion on this journey.**

ALL **All-powerful God, you always show mercy to those who love you and you are never far away from those who seek you. Remain with us on our pilgrimage of faith and guide our way in accord with your will. Shelter us by day, give us the light of your knowledge by night, and as our companion on the journey, bring us to all destinations in safety. Through Christ our Lord. Amen.**

SOURCES AND FOR MORE

For more, the two best places to go are, be not surprised, Church documents:

Decree on the Apostolate of the Laity (*Apostolicam Actuositatem*), Vatican II, November 18, 1965
> This is easy-to-read in one sitting, and holds much of the key to what the Second Vatican Council was about.

The Lay Members of Christ's Faithful People (*Christifideles Laici*), Post-Synodal Apostolic Exhortation on the Vocation and Mission of the Lay Faithful in the Church and in the World, Pope St. John Paul II, December 30, 1988
> This could reasonably be called the Lay Catholic version of books such as The Boy Scout Handbook.

Page 5, *The Catechism...*, **Catechism of the Catholic Church, 2nd Edition**, promulgated by Pope St. John Paul II, 1997, Visit www.vatican.va

Page 8, *Pope John Paul II had given us...*, **I Will Give You Shepherds (*Pastores Dabo Vobis*)**, Pope St. John Paul II, March 25, 1992

Page 9, *Books on masculine spirituality...*, (and other books):
- **He: Understanding Masculine Psychology**, Robert A. Johnson, Harper & Row, 1989
- **King, Warrior, Magician, Lover: Rediscovering the Archetypes of the Mature Masculine**, Robert Moore and Douglas Gillette, Harper Collins, 1990
- **The Masculine Spirit: Resources for Reflective Living**, Max Oliva, Ave Maria Press, 1997
- **Sacraments: Rites of Passage**, William J. O'Malley, S.J. Thomas More Publishing, 1995
- **The Quest for the Male Soul**, Martin Pable, Capuchin, Ave Maria Press, 1996

Adam's Return: the Five Promises of Male Initiation, Richard Rohr, O.F.M. Crossroad Publishing, 2004

Men and Women: The Journey of Spiritual Transformation (Two Talks on Tape), Richard Rohr, O.F.M., St. Anthony Messenger Press, 1999

The Holy Longing: the Search for a Christian Spirituality, Ronald Rohlheiser, O.M.I., Doubleday, 1999

The Rites of Passage, Arnold Van Gennep, University of Chicago Press, 1960

Page 9, *the little book…*, **The Wild Man's Journey: Revised Edition**, Richard Rohr, OFM, and Joseph Martos, St. Anthony Messenger Press, 1996

> If you know a man who seems to be floundering, stick this book in next year's Christmas stocking. No kidding.
> For a woman? **The Inner Voice of Love** by Henri Nouwen.

Page 16, *As Christ was anointed Priest, Prophet, and King…*, **Rite of Baptism for Children**, ICEL, 1969, Catholic Book Publishing Company, Inc., 1970-1977

Page 18, *Blessing Sons and Daughters…*, adapted from *Blessing of Sons and Daughters* in **Book of Blessings**, ICEL, 1987, Catholic Book Publishing Co., 1989

> The prayer used is appropriate for anyone, but there is another at paragraph 190 which is specially for parents, tracing a cross on their children's forehead:
>
> ***Father**, inexhaustible source of life and author of all good, we bless you and we thank you for brightening our communion of love by your gift of children. Grant that our children (child) will find in the life of this family such inspiration that they (he/she) will strive always for what is right and good and one day, by your grace, reach their (his/her) home in heaven. Through Christ our Lord. Amen.*

Page 22, **Schindler's List**, the story of Oskar Schindler, directed by Steven Spielberg, 1993

Page 23, ...*not a single vocation among us which was not once a priestly one...*, **Secular Sanctity: Reflections on Finding God in the Midst of Daily Life**, Edward Hays, Forest of Peace Publishing, 1984

> The 17 chapters of this one was a great source for a year of adult faith formation led by adult catechists.

Page 29, *The child-like spirituality...*, also on pages 47, 63, and 80, was inspired by St. Leo the Great, from a 1991 **Rite of Baptism Booklet** by Catholic Book Publishing Co., has been taped inside the back of my Baptism ritual book for twenty years now.

Page 30, ...*a good corporation...a priest...*, **Corporate Cultures: the Rites and Rituals of Corporate Life**, Terrence E. Deal and Allan A. Kennedy, Basic Books, 1982

> Deal and Kennedy continued to update their teachings. Working at a CPA firm, I found this idea provocative, but began noticing priestly presences at the firm and at clients.

Page 31, *No peace without justice; no justice without forgiveness...*, Pope Saint John Paul II, *Message for the Celebration of the World Day of Peace*, January 1, 2012

> John Paul II builds on *If you want peace, work for justice...*, Pope Paul VI, *Message for the Celebration of the Day of Peace*, January 1, 1972, also attributed to H.L. Mencken, d. 1956, perhaps a wise antidote to the Latin maxim, *If you want peace, prepare for war.*

Page 32, *Blessing the Sick...*, adapted from *Orders for the Blessing of the Sick* in **Book of Blessings**, ICEL, 1987, Catholic Book Publishing Co., 1989

Page 40, *Recognizing the violence in my heart...*, **The Pax Christi Pledge of Nonviolence**, www.paxchristiusa.org

SOURCES and FOR MORE

Page 44, ...*provocative nonviolence*..., **Catholicism**, Robert Barron, www.wordonfire.org
> There is a place in Bishop Barron's video series where he calls us to pray for creativity in using nonviolence in the way that Gandhi and Martin Luther King, Jr. did. But my favorite work by this great teacher is still
> **The Strangest Way: Walking the Christian Path**, Robert Barron, Orbis Books, 2002

Page 48, *Consider: one chapter-a-day takes 44 months...*, For other reading plans, visit www.idjc.org.

Page 32, *Blessing Learners and Teachers...*, adapted from *Order for the Blessing of Students and Teachers* in **Book of Blessings**, ICEL, 1987, Catholic Book Publishing Co., 1989

Page 55, *And the work Adam and Eve would have done in the garden was worship...*, **The New Man**, Thomas Merton, The Noonday Press, 1961, page 80:
> *Adam's work was worship...*
> *Our work ought to be a dialogue with reality,*
> *and therefore a conversation with God.*

Page 57, *Mature disciples...*, **Stewardship: A Disciple's Response**, U.S. Bishops, 1992

Page 58, **The Quotidian Mysteries: Laundry, Liturgy, and "Women's Work"** (Madeleva Lecture in Spirituality), Kathleen Norris, Paulist Press, May 1, 1998

Page 59, ...*the gift of royal freedom*..., **Constitution on the Church in the Modern World (*Lumen Gentium*)**, Second Vatican Council, November 21, 1964, www.vatican.va

Page 60, *and only Yes to God*..., See **New Seeds of Contemplation**, Thomas Merton, New Directions, 1961, pg 199
> *Perfect spiritual freedom is a total inability*
> *to make any evil choice.*

Page 60, *The Principle and Foundation*, Paragraph 23 of **Spiritual Exercises**, Saint Ignatius of Loyola, d. 1556
> The Principle and Foundation is usually part of the first days of an Jesuit retreat, where we are asked to sit with the truth that God loves us, we sin, and God still loves us.

Page 64, *Blessing Victims of Addiction & Violence...*, adapted from *Order for the Blessing of a Person Suffering from Addiction or from Substance Abuse* and *Order for the Blessing of a Victim of Crime or Oppression* in **Book of Blessings**, ICEL, 1987, Catholic Book Publishing Co., 1989

Page 69, *Don't you believe that God will make you what God created you to be...*, **The Seven Storey Mountain**, Thomas Merton, Harcourt Brace and Company, 1948, page 238

Page 69, *Decades later...*, **New Seeds of Contemplation**, Thomas Merton, New Directions, 1961, page 39:
> *No natural exercise can bring you into vital contact with God. Unless God utters Godself in you, **speaks God's own name in the center of your soul**, you will no more know God than a stone knows the ground upon which it rests in its inertia... We become contemplatives when God discovers Godself in us.*

Page 72, *Nowhere in the bible does it say...*, **One Like Jesus: Conversations on the Single Life**, Debra K. Farrington, John Wiley & Sons, 1999

Page 73, *Many people who are unmarried...*, **The Joy of Love (*Amoris Laetitia*)**, Pope Francis, 2016

Page 75, *Modern married life is complicated...*, **The Springs of Contemplation: A Retreat at the Abbey of Gethsemani** in December 1967 and May 1968, Thomas Merton, Ave Maria Press, 1992, page 86

SOURCES and FOR MORE

Page 75, *Being single is…*, **The Called and Gifted Workshop of the Catherine of Siena Institute**, www.siena.org

Page 81, *Retrouvaille…*, I have seen miracles happen to marriages in trouble who gave **Retrouvaille** a shot: Tell all your married friends: **www.retrouvaille.org** For another model of stages of a marriage, see **Being Spouses: from celibate observation**, Stephen Joseph Wolf, idjc press, 2014

Page 82, *Blessing Families…*, adapted from *Order for the Blessing of a Family* in **Book of Blessings**, ICEL, 1987, Catholic Book Publishing Co., 1989

Page 91, *A very important acknowledgement…*, **The Called and Gifted Workshop of the Catherine of Siena Institute**, Sherry Anne Weddell, Fr. Michael Sweeney, O.P., and all the other good folks of the Catherine of Siena Institute. Go **to www.siena.org** and find one of their workshops. If you can't make it to one yet, run to the bookstore and order Sherry A. Weddell's **Fruitful Discipleship: Living the Mission of Jesus in the Church and the World**, Our Sunday Visitor, 2017

Page 94, *Organization…*, This chart is compiled from my studies of the charisms through the Catherine of Siena Institute and helping parishioners discern charisms for a number of years. It is just a taste!

Page 99, *Lay faithful are on the front lines…*, *Discourse to the New Cardinals*, Pope Pius XII, 1946, quoted in ***Christifideles Laici***, Pope Saint John Paul II, 1988

Page 102, *Blessing Pilgrims…*, adapted from *Order for the Blessing of Pilgrims on their Departure* in **Book of Blessings**, ICEL, 1987, Catholic Book Publishing Co., 1989

Priest Prophet King, DVD, two discs, 162 minutes, Rated G, Bishop Robert Barron, www.WordOnFire.org, 2014:
1. Adoratio
2. The High Priest
3. Challenging False Worship
4. The Word Made Flesh
5. Ordering the Kingdom
6. King of Kings

Go deeper in your baptismal identity in Christ Jesus, the Priest, Prophet, and King. Bishop Barron weaves these Old Testament identities in the person of Jesus, fully God and fully human. You will enjoy spending some time with perhaps the best teacher of my life.

Fruitful Discipleship: Living the Mission of Jesus in the Church and the World, Sherry A. Weddell, Our Sunday Visitor, 2017, 232 pages:
1. The Weight of My Neighbor's Glory
2. Where's the Fruit?
3. The Undaunted Fruit-Farmer
4. The Charismatic Is Co-Essential
5. Charisms 101
6. Pastoral and Communications Charisms
7. Organizational and Lifestyle Charisms
8. Healing, Understanding, and Creative Charisms
9. The Art of Discerning Charisms
10. Facing Outward

As I say in the text of God's Ones, I am profoundly grateful for the work of Sherry Anne Weddell and the Catherine of Siena Institute. This delightful book is graced with insights from two decades of her work with faithful Catholics and discernment of Charisms.

FOR MORE

Pay a visit to **www.siena.org/called-gifted.**

The **Called & Gifted**™ discernment process helps people recognize the charisms given to them at baptism that equip them to live out their call in the world.

Step One is the Called and Gifted workshop, which lays the foundation for the beginning of discernment.

Step Two is a one hour gifts interview, an invaluable part of the process. (It usually take me 90 minutes to do this.)

Step Three helps you begin discernment in the real world. It will teach you how to
- develop charism experiments
- evaluate your results
- identify ways you learned to control life as a child that get in the way of using your charisms as an adult.

If you are unable to get to a Called and Gifted workshop, you can also purchase
Called & Gifted Complete Materials for Individuals
for $60 at www.siena.org/bookstore, which includes:
- Called & Gifted I: 4-CD set
- Called & Gifted II: 3-CD set
- Resource Guide
- Catholic Spiritual Gifts Inventory
- Discerning Charisms Workbook.

And you can schedule a 1 hour phone gifts interview for $40.

This is how I was first introduced to charisms when serving as Director of Vocation Formation for the Diocese of Nashville. It is a bit like going to the horse races and getting all your racing forms from one place. If you are serious about your faith, you will thoroughly enjoy it!

Blessings,
Steve Wolf

www.ingramcontent.com/pod-product-compliance
Lightning Source LLC
Chambersburg PA
CBHW021155080526
44588CB00008B/355